BOOKED

literature in the soul of me

To Pessy,
Thank you for spending
some time with the
books,
Karen Swallow Prior

k a r e n   s w a l l o w   p r i o r

ts T. S. Poetry Press • New York

T. S. Poetry Press
Ossining, New York
Tspoetry.com

This book includes references to the following brands and sources: "American Pie" is from the album *American Pie* by Don McLean, United Artists, 1971; *Are You There God? It's Me, Margaret* is by Judy Blume, Yearling, 1950; "Rape Fantasies" is by Margaret Atwood, originally published in *Dancing Girls*, 1977; *Go Ask Alice* is by an anonymous author, Prentice Hall, 1971; *That Was Then, This is Now* and *The Outsiders* are by S. E. Hinton, Viking/Penguin, 1971 and 1967; *Harry Potter* is a copyright of Bloomsbury Publishers; *Twilight* is by Stephanie Meyer, copyright Little, Brown and Company; *King of the Wind* is by Marguerite Henry, Rand McNally, 1948; Sears Back-to-School Catalogue, Christmas Wishbook, and Sears Kenmore are copyrights of Sears Roebuck and Co.; *Middlemarch* is by George Eliot, William Blackwood and Sons, 1871; *Humpty Dumpty Potato Chips* are a trademark of Humpty Dumpty Snack Foods; *Endgame* is a play by Samuel Beckett which opened at the Royal Court Theatre in 1957; *The Blue Lagoon* is a movie released through Columbia Pictures, 1980; *Fear of Flying* is by Erica Jong, Holt, Rinehart and Winston, 1973; Star Wars is a copyright of Lucasfilm Limited; *Beauty and the Beast* is a film by Walt Disney Animation Studios; Sybil is by Flora Rheta Schrebier, Regnery 1973; *Dr. Seuss' The Foot Book* is by Theodor Geisel, 1968; *Richard Scarry's Busy, Busy World* is by Richard Scarry published by Goldencraft, 1970; *The Mouse and the Motorcycle* is by Beverly Cleary, HarperTrophy, 1965; *Clifford the Big Red Dog* is by Norman Bridewell, published by Scholastic Books in 1963; *Casey The Utterly Impossible Horse* is by Anita MacRae Feagles, published by Scholastic Books in 1962; *Harriet the Spy* is by Lousie Fitzhugh, Harper and Row, 1964; *Ramona the Brave* is by Beverly Cleary, William Morrow, 1975; the Nancy Drew series was created by publisher Edward Stratemeyer; *Charlie and the Chocolate Factory* is by Roald Dahl, Alfred A. Knopf, 1964; *Where the Red Fern Grows* is by Wilson Rawls, Doubleday, 1961; *The Black Stallion* is by Walter Farley, Random House, 1941; *Pippi Longstocking* is by Astrid Lindgren, Viking Press, 1950; *The Lion, The Witch, and The Wardrobe* is by C. S. Lewis, Geoffrey Bles, 1950; *Tiger Beat* is a publication of Laufer Media, Inc.

Cover image by Kelly Langner Sauer. kellysauer.com

Names, identifying features, and events have been altered and in some cases compressed for the sake of both narrative flow and protection of others' privacy.

ISBN 978-0-692-01454-7

Library of Congress Cataloging-in-Publication Data:
Prior, Karen Swallow
        [Memoir.]
        Booked: Literature in the soul of me/Karen Swallow Prior
        ISBN 978-0-692-01454-7
        Library of Congress Control Number: 2012952180

In memory of Mrs. Lovejoy
for offering her students
Great Expectations

TABLE OF CONTENTS

1 Books Promiscuously Read:
   John Milton's *Areopagitica*   9

2 The Life-Giving Power of Words:
   Charlotte's Web   27

3 God of the Awkward, the Freckled, and the Strange:
   Gerard Manley Hopkins's "Pied Beauty"   45

4 The Magic of Story:
   Great Expectations   55

5 Beholding is Becoming:
   Jane Eyre   71

6 The Only Thing Between Me and Tragedy:
   Tess of the D'Urbervilles   95

7 Sex, Symbol, and Satire:
   Gulliver's Travels   117

8 Know Thyself:
   Death of a Salesman   139

9 The Fate of the Romantic:
   Madame Bovary   159

10 Real Love is Like a Compass:
   John Donne's Metaphysical Poetry   179

11 Welcoming Wonder:
   The Poetry of Doubt   189

Discussion Questions   200

1

Books Promiscuously Read: John Milton's *Areopagitica*

> Tell all the Truth but tell it slant —
> Success in Circuit lies
> Too bright for our infirm Delight
> The Truth's superb surprise
>
> As Lightning to the Children eased
> With explanation kind
> The Truth must dazzle gradually
> Or every man be blind —
>
> —Emily Dickinson

My fingers slid across smooth book spines, skimming the familiar titles lined up on the shelf, firmly and tightly, like little soldiers standing at attention. Soon I spotted the name of an old friend: *King of the Wind* by Marguerite Henry. It had been many, many years since I'd read this book—the tale of a royal Arabian horse and the adventures he shared around the world with a Moroccan stable boy named Agba—and countless other horse stories by Henry. It had been nearly as many years, too, since I'd stood in this space, a nearly sacred place, the library of my childhood. Maybe it really was sacred, the reliquary of my soul.

The relics, these books on the shelves in this quiet alcove, brought me here, a small-town public library nestled in the corner of a building not unlike a cathedral. Cumston Hall is a Romanesque Revival style edifice of gothic proportions, built at the turn of the century as a gift to the town of Monmouth, Maine, from Dr. Charles M. Cumston, who had been a teacher at the first public high school in America. When I was growing up in this town, I thought of Cumston Hall as an enchanted castle, a place filled with history and story and mystery. It was home not only to all of these books, but also to a seasonal theater company that brought to life many of the stories within the pages of these books, to stuffy town meetings that sucked the life right back out, and to luminous stained-glass windows, mysterious winding stairwells, jutting balconies, mural-laden walls, ceilings painted with glorious cloud-cushioned cherubim, and—naturally—rumors of haunting ghosts. The library ensconced its children's books in a tower-like room, which made browsing the books—hugging those lucky ones chosen to be carried home for a spell—all the more magical.

The power of these books brought me, not only back to this physical space but also to this place in my life, for on this trip I was returning to my hometown and to the library of my youth as a doctoral candidate in English literature, a life centered professionally on books. But my relationship with books was much more than professional; it was—is—personal. Deeply personal. Books have formed the soul of me.

I know that spiritual formation is of God, but I also know—mainly because I learned it from books—that there are other kinds of formation, too, everyday gifts, and that God uses the things of this earth to teach us and shape us, and to help us find truth. One such gift is that my soul was entrusted to two good parents, one a mother who loves books and who read consistently to her children as we were growing up. Just as weekly attendance at church and Sunday school was part of what it meant to belong to my family, so too was my mother reading to each of us, my two older brothers and me, every night at bedtime. These rituals were part of our lives well past the age when most of my friends were no longer tucked into bed, or read to, or made to go to church by their parents. Even into my brothers' teen years our mother made the rounds to each separate bedroom, reading a section nightly from books of our choosing.

I'm not sure when we felt we had outgrown the bedtime stories, but I do know that my brothers and I each came to feel we had outgrown church. The bedtime stories, however, ceased long before compulsory church attendance did. Even friends or cousins who slept over on Saturday night knew they would be attending church with our family come Sunday morning. For most of them, this was the only time they ever went to church, so naturally, I was apologetic. And embarrassed. We New Englanders may derive from Puritan stock, but the stoic independence more than the religious piety has survived into the current age. I made up to my friends by entertaining them during the service: snickering at the drops of spittle that seeped from one corner of the pastor's mouth while he preached, making naughty puns on the names of the parishioners, and singing the hymns in a high, quavering old lady voice only the friend next to me could hear. Anyone needing evidence of the human soul's need for formation need look no further than a sneering child seated on a church pew on a Sunday morn.

Although being raised by God-loving parents is no guarantee that one will love God oneself, it certainly helps. I did love God, even if it didn't always show, but for much of my life, I loved books more than God, never discovering for a long, long time that a God who spoke the world into existence with words is, in fact, the source of meaning of all words. My journey toward that discovery is the story of this book. I thought my love of books was taking me away from God, but as it turns out, books were the backwoods path back to God, bramble-filled and broken, yes, but full of truth and wonder.

Books and the reading of books fill the memories of my early childhood as much as anything else. My childhood rituals of reading encompassed a complicated set of ceremonies, rules, and traditions not unlike those of the church. One rare occasion, my mother being out, my father put me to bed. While reading me my requisite bedtime story, he arrived at a place in the book where my mother, instead of reading the words *sniff, sniff,* would instead make the sound of sniffing. My poor father, ignorant of this particular tradition, made the mistake of saying the words, "sniff, sniff," and suffered a haughty correction from me.

I learned to read on my own with Dr. Seuss' *The Foot Book,* in my room, using a finger to trace each word as I sounded it out.

An older playmate nearby, engrossed silently in another book, gave me an exasperated "Shhhh!" as I pronounced every word. Indignant at being shushed while carrying out such a significant task as reading by myself, I soldiered on, whispering,

> *In the house,*
> *and on the street,*
> *how many, many*
> *feet you meet.*

I remember the titles, pictures, and the words of so many favorite books: the colorful chaos of Richard Scarry's *Busy, Busy World*; the tale of Ralph, the rodent with the helmet made of half a pingpong ball in *The Mouse and the Motorcycle*; the adventures of the mutt every child wishes were her own, *Clifford the Big Red Dog*; *Casey The Utterly Impossible Horse*, that contradicts every girl's horse fantasy; the story of the inimitable and enviable anti-hero *Harriet the Spy*; that tomboy of tomboys, *Ramona the Brave*; the smart and sassy Nancy Drew series; the delightful and whimsical *Charlie and the Chocolate Factory*; *Where the Red Fern Grows*, which left me weeping inconsolably the night I finished it, alone, lying in the top bunk of my bedroom; my favorite horse book ever, *The Black Stallion*; and *Pippi Longstocking*. I secretly liked that my dad's special nickname for me was "Pippi" because of my own freckles and pigtails. I didn't even point out to my father that my pigtails didn't stick straight out like Pippi's did. I remember *The Lion, The Witch, and The Wardrobe*. Ever since, I have loved wardrobes so much that my own home is furnished with as many as I can reasonably fit.

Some of these titles were among those I scanned all these years later in the library at Cumston Hall. By now many new titles by more recent authors I'd never heard of overwhelmed the old, familiar titles. I smiled to think of young readers who loved these new books and who would be eager to spread their love of the stories to others, as I had done with my beloved books as a child.

One summer, when I was about seven, I was inspired to share my love of reading and my own books with everyone I could.

Everyone at the time consisted of the twins next door and a few other kids on the neighboring blocks. I made my own lending library out of the basement of our little Cape Cod bungalow in the suburbs of Buffalo, where we lived for a few years when my father was transferred from his office in Maine. I borrowed a rickety little bookcase, one constructed of particleboard my mother had covered with a contact paper made to look like real wood, except that it was gray, not brown. I organized my books on the shelves according to reading level and author, designed homemade library cards, and invited all my friends over to traipse down the basement stairs and crowd around that bookcase to make their selections. How vividly I remember that day! Glowing, I checked out each book and bestowed upon my friends what I knew to be the source of one of the greatest joys in the world.

I have little memory of the succeeding days of my library, short-lived as they surely were. Although my friends humored me for a spell, I don't think they were nearly as excited about my library as I was. I'm not even sure whether I ever got all my books back.

Eventually, my Uncle Bobby moved into the basement after he dropped out of college. He brought his own library with him— a library of records shelved on a real record store display rack. He let me pick up the albums and examine the cover art and pore over the song titles. I liked to memorize the titles and artists the same way I memorized books and their authors. And Uncle Bobby would play songs for me when I asked him. My favorite song was "American Pie" by Don McLean, which had a line in it about the Father, Son, and the Holy Ghost and another about taking a Chevy to a levy. I knew what a Chevy was because my father wouldn't buy one, but I didn't know what a levy was; I just liked the rhyme. Uncle Bobby was pretty cool even if he liked records better than books. I came to appreciate records, too.

Like the culture that grows organisms in a petri dish, popular music, movies, and, for some more than others, books cultivate modern adolescents. Like many American, pre-pubescent girls, my sense of what it meant to be a girl-becoming-woman was greatly influenced by one author in particular: Judy Blume.

There's nothing like *Are You There God? It's Me, Margaret* to get a girl excited about menstruation or—in the case of an embarrassingly-late bloomer like me—absolutely mortified at being the last of one's friends to be sanctified by the rite of menarche. This momentous event was so much on the minds of my middle school friends that when one of them—the first girl in my class to get her hair cut like Farrah Fawcett's and who, like Margaret in the book was Jewish, the only Jewish girl in my school, in fact—ran up to me between classes one day, waving a piece of paper, she didn't have to say a word. The page was entirely blank except for a small dot she had penned into the middle. Farrah Hair and I both screamed and hugged each other in raptures of joy.

Well, only one of us was joyous, actually, and it wasn't me. As if always being one of the last ones picked for teams during gym class wasn't bad enough, now it seemed I was going to be the last one on Team Period, too.

At least I had books. Church stifled me; my friends and their blossoming bodies, and the boys that flocked around them were all leaving me behind; but books made my world feel bigger and made me feel freer. Some of these books took me to places most people would say a young girl shouldn't go, but my parents never restricted my reading, unlike many parents today who seem to spend a lot of time fretting over what to allow their kids to read or not to read.

It seems to me to be an entirely negative, not to mention ineffective, strategy to shield children from reality rather than actively expose them to the sort of truth that emerges organically from the give-and-take of weighing and reckoning competing ideas against one another. Discovering truth is a process that occurs over time, more fully with each idea or book that gets added to the equation. Sure, many of the books I read in my youth filled my head with silly notions and downright lies that I mistook for truth, but only until I read something else that exposed the lie for what it was.

Books meet with disapproval because of their objectionable content. Wisdom, however, considers not only what a book says (its content), but how it says it (its form). Just as important—

or perhaps more important than—whether a book contains questionable themes like sex or violence or drugs or witchcraft or candy is how those topics are portrayed. Are they presented truthfully in terms of their context and their consequences? Are dangerous actions, characters, or ideas glamorized in a way that makes them enticing? Are the bad guys presented with so much sympathy that the reader tends to identify with them? Are the good guys so insipid that you couldn't imagine having lunch with one of them, let alone having one as your friend? Discerning judgments of literature consider form as much as content, just as with any other art.

The funny thing is that the only time I can remember hearing anything in church about the form and content of art is when an old time preacher and youth evangelist who was sort of a local legend came to speak at our church. The topic of his sermon was the Evils of Rock Music. As it turns out, rock music is evil not only because of the content of its lyrics but because of the form of its music: rhythmic beats originating from the African jungle designed to simulate (and stimulate) the sex act. Listening to the old geezer go on about such things, I was both mortified and fascinated. Even at sixteen, I recognized the basis of the argument as little more than sketchy research and pseudo-science. By this time I was no longer bringing my cousins and friends to church with me after Saturday night sleepovers, but I couldn't help but wish some of them were there to snicker with me. Instead, all of the other youth group kids seemed to be soaking it up like it was the gospel truth.

The next time my youth leaders had an overnighter at their home, the husband took us up to his attic—it wasn't a real attic, mind you, but kind of a cubby hole built into the side of an upstairs room—and told us that he had taken all the albums from his youth that he had once stored there and burned them. My Uncle Bobby had long ago moved out from our house and started a family of his own and so no longer lived with us, but I wondered still what he would have thought of this record-burning business. I wondered if "American Pie" was among the youth leader's burnt offerings, but then I figured his taste probably wasn't that good. I had come to understand by now that the "American Pie" wasn't literally about the Father, Son, and Holy Ghost, but that only made it all the more brilliant. Soon after this night, I stopped going to youth group altogether and spent more time getting high.

They'd probably have kicked me out anyway, if they knew about the books I read. And the music I listened to. And the pot I smoked. Or worse, they'd have given me an earnest lecture.

Not long ago, in my present life as a college administrator and English professor, the parent of a freshman came to me to complain about a story being taught in his daughter's literature class. The story was "Rape Fantasies" by Margaret Atwood. It's a humorous story about a serious topic, and the gist of it is that in coping with the ever-present possibility of rape in our lives, women think about what they would do or how they would handle such a threat if it arose. The fact that the characters don't think about rape in very realistic terms only emphasizes just how unthinkable such a thing is.

Well, this father was having none of it. He feared the story might lead male students to think women want to be raped and that it was traumatic for female students (namely, his daughter) to read. He would not allow her to read it, and he thought the professors in my department shouldn't be assigning it to students. He had read it because, he explained to me, he read all of his daughter's assignments before she did and blacked out with a marker anything he thought she shouldn't read. He thought this entire story needed to be blacked out; I wish I were making this up.

"But rape is a very real threat that women have to live with and think about," I tried to explain.

"Not my wife or daughter," he shot back. "They don't have to think about it."

I could see that the conversation was going nowhere. This man needed a reality check. "Well, I fantasize about rape every day," I said.

He squirmed in his chair and looked down. "I don't need to know about that," he muttered.

"Why, yes, you do," I answered, my voice growing firm. "You see, I'm a runner, and I live out in the country where I have to decide every day whether or not I want to run on the main road, trafficked by logging trucks, or on a quiet, deserted dirt road. Most days, I choose the dirt road. And on the rare occasion when a vehicle comes down that road, I pay attention. I know all the regulars by heart, and if an unfamiliar one approaches, I think about which way I'll head through the woods if I need to, and I keep my phone at the ready. That's what I fantasize about every day."

He was quiet for a moment, but a very short one. "Well, my daughter doesn't need to worry about that."

"But someday when she's out walking on the street at night, alone, she will," I insisted. What would this man think, I wondered, if he knew that when I was seventeen and came home from school one day and told my parents that my health teacher had been propositioning me—in class—my parents didn't intervene. They expected me to take care of the matter on my own and that if I couldn't, only then would I come back to them for help.

I took care of it myself.

"No, she won't. Because she will never be out walking the street at night alone," he said, shaking his head. "I'll never let her do that."

And to that there was nothing I could really say.

What might such a parent think of the kinds of books I had read at a far younger age? For example, *Go Ask Alice,* a work so controversial that it has earned a permanent and prominent place on the American Library Association's list of the 100 Most Frequently Challenged Books. I read a lot of the books on that list as I was growing up, never even knowing that such a list existed, but this book remains memorable to me because it was the only one I recall raising a parental eyebrow.

After snooping around in my oldest brother's bedroom one day, I found the book—a supposed diary of a teenager who ultimately dies of an overdose weeks after the last entry in a journal chronicling two years in and out of the abyss of drug abuse—and stole away with it. At some point in the book, I stumbled across a word I didn't know. Since my mother had intentionally cultivated a relationship between us that was open and honest, and she had always encouraged me to come to her with any questions about anything at all, I naturally felt free to ask,

"Mom, what is o-r-g-a-s-m?"

To my surprise, she didn't answer. My mom always answered my questions. Instead, she asked, "What are you reading?"

When I showed her, she said, hesitatingly, "I don't know if you should be reading that."

"Well, I'm almost done with it anyway," I answered, as matter-of-factly as I could and slinked off to finish reading it before she could pursue that line of thinking any further.

Later, I looked up the word in the dictionary. I still didn't get it.

Of course, it's words like that, along with the book's depictions of sexual promiscuity, rape, and drug abuse that garner it so much attention from the book-banning crowd. But herein lies a perfect example of how ideas are portrayed is just as (if not more) important than what ideas are portrayed. No one believes that *Go Ask Alice* is the real diary of a real teen. I'm not even sure I fell for that trick at the age of eleven. Rather, the book is pretty clearly a pretty clever—over 4 million copies have been sold since its first publication in 1971—work of anti-drug propaganda. And it worked, for the time being, on me. It's a bit ironic, then, that this was the only book my mother ever expressed concern about my reading.

On the other hand, while *Go Ask Alice* effectively scared me off drugs at least through my middle school years (which was more of a feat than it might seem), another book which is highly favored among teachers and critics made drugs and drug abusers seem downright glamorous: S. E. Hinton's *That Was Then, This is Now.* I was introduced to this book by the first in Hinton's series, *The Outsiders,* the gateway book to the harder stuff. Gosh, Ponyboy Curtis, Johnny Cade and M&M all seemed so cool. When next I read *That Was Then, This is Now,* I wrote a book report for my fifth grade teacher that turned into a rhapsody extending pages beyond the required length for the assignment. I've wondered since then what my teacher must have thought upon reading that book report, but whatever it was, she kept it to herself, which seems a bit odd given how exuberantly I expressed my admiration for these drug-imbibing scofflaws. I was in love with M&M and was sure that I could have saved him from overdosing on LSD.

Fifth-graders just know these things. I certainly knew these things. After all, this was also the year that the school separated out the boys and the girls one day and showed each group of us The Film. After that, we knew pretty much everything, even things we might not have wanted to know.

And this is exactly why—many people would say—young people shouldn't read books like *That Was Then, This is Now*. Such books give us the wrong ideas. They certainly gave me the wrong ideas. I carried some of those concepts around in my head for a good long time. My infatuation with a drugged-out little juvenile delinquent would eventually render all the nice boys in my church's youth group utterly undateable. They weren't dangerous enough. Or perhaps they weren't needy enough. Or both.

Was the helicopter parent who objected to his daughter's college reading assignments right? Wouldn't I have been better off if I'd never been exposed to such notions at all?

Well, if I'd stopped reading then and there, perhaps so. But I didn't stop reading. I read more and more books and, by exposure to so many competing ideas and examples, I gained a more truthful understanding of the nature of love and life and relationships—and drugs—and so much more.

This is why books should be "promiscuously read."

These are the words of John Milton in his famous 1644, anti-censorship tract, *Areopagitica*. In the midst of the English Civil Wars, when the price for a wrongheaded idea might well be one's head, Milton argued passionately in this treatise that the best way to counteract falsehood is not by suppressing it, but by countering it with truth. The essence of Milton's argument is that truth is stronger than falsehood; falsehood prevails through the suppression of countering ideas, but truth triumphs in a free and open exchange that allows truth to shine. This was, I think, the essence of my parents' approach to their children's reading, though they didn't express it this way. My parents hadn't ever read Milton, but they had good instincts and a good dose of common sense.

I learned about John Milton and his most famous work, *Paradise Lost*, in college, but I wasn't introduced to *Areopagitica* until graduate school. Oddly enough, even then it wasn't in a class but through a remarkable series of events.

I had taken a couple of classes with a professor who seemed to me to be one of the most liberal, perverse, and intellectually intimidating people I had ever known. I read my first (and last) work of pornography as an assignment in his class (it was eighteenth-century pornography, but pornography nonetheless. *Go Ask Alice* was nothing compared to this!). It seemed as if this professor was always saying the wickedest things, and I could never tell if he was serious or if he just thought that being provocative was part of a professor's job within one of the most liberal departments in a liberal state university.

One evening, while conducting a make-up class in his home, the professor regaled the grad students with tales of shocking his undergraduates in a course he taught on the First Amendment. One of his favorite tactics was to show them the "homoerotic" photographs of the acclaimed and controversial photographer Robert Mapplethorpe. When the professor mockingly described the indignation of "some redneck born again" student, I called him out. In front of everyone. I didn't think it likely that it was only the "born again" undergrads that were queasy about seeing photographs of men with various implements plunged into their bodily orifices.

"Surely, you're not stereotyping?" I asked with as sophisticated a tone of sarcasm as I could muster. He was my professor, after all. I tried to sound cool and cynical and disinterested, but my insides were bubbling up. I had been in graduate school long enough to have sensed less-than-warm attitudes by many toward religious belief in general and Christianity in particular. I had not tried to hide my faith, but I had understood that it was best not to wear it on my sleeve either. I certainly had never confronted a professor about the bias I had seen both in and out of the classroom. Perhaps meeting in the professor's home, in the relaxed comfort of the living room where we were casually circled, I felt a freedom I'm sure I'd have never felt in the classroom.

The room was dimly lit and I was grateful for this as I felt my face crimson. I don't remember exactly my professor's or my fellow students' immediate reaction, but from the professor I think it was something along the lines of a terse admission and apology, followed by a quick change of subject. What followed once the class was over is seared in my memory. On my way out, the professor stopped me at the door and offered a genuine, more profuse apology for what he acknowledged was a serious transgression against the liberal values he espoused. I had to respect him for both striving to be consistent with his own profession for tolerance and for admitting failure when he wasn't. All the other students had left, and we spoke for about twenty minutes. A new understanding and mutual respect between us took root.

From this day on, my professor would often ask my view of topics in class, explaining to the others, respectfully, that he was particularly seeking my view as a Christian, thus paying more than lip service (unlike many of his peers) to the diversity and tolerance he valued. But many times my professor would talk to me more after class, sitting in the stifling space of his tiny office—it and hundreds others like it were part of the campus's riot-proof architectural design, developed after the student protests of the sixties and epitomizing modernism's cold, utilitarian, de-humanized aesthetics. We discussed Christianity and Christians, liberalism and liberals, conservatism and conservatives, free speech and John Milton—and the surprising role that a conservative, Puritan Christian had in developing one of the most cherished cornerstones of American freedom.

While Milton wrote *Areopagitica* in a context far removed both chronologically and politically from the U. S. Constitution, his argument against the licensing orders of the seventeenth-century English government was instrumental in the thinking that shaped the First Amendment. Milton's stance is even more significant when one considers that he was arguing against the policies of his own Puritan faction. Milton demonstrated the universal power of truth not only in the content of his treatise, but also in the very act of countering his fellow Christians: by standing for truth even against his own party, Milton embodied the very power of truth. Milton thus exemplifies the person of integrity whose allegiance is to truth rather than comfort, to doctrine rather than political or social expediency. Like my professor turned out to be.

Even outside of Milton's context as a seventeenth-century Puritan, his argument for promiscuous reading is instructive, because such an approach is still both the means and the mark of the intellectually- and spiritually-mature person. If only that father who brandished the black marker against his daughter's college textbooks had read—and received—Milton's wisdom.

Today the word *promiscuous* is usually associated with sexual behavior, but this is a more recent usage, one that comes from the word's actual meaning—*indiscriminate mixing*. It's easy to see the sexual application of the word from this definition but instructive to think about in the context of reading. It's surprising, I think, to realize that pious and scholarly Milton is actually arguing for indiscriminate, disorderly reading. And lots of it. In Milton's day people had more fears surrounding promiscuous reading than promiscuous sex (the latter being rarer), so Milton had quite the challenge ahead of him.

In making his argument, as a churchman speaking to fellow churchmen, Milton cites the biblical examples of Moses, Daniel, and Paul, who were all steeped in the writings of their surrounding pagan cultures. Milton also invokes a leader of the third-century church who asserted that God commanded him in a vision, "Read any books whatever come into your hands, for you are sufficient both to judge aright and to examine each matter." Such advice mirrors the Pauline suggestion to "test all things and hold fast to that which is good." Milton puts it most profoundly when he says,

> Well knows he who uses to consider, that our faith and knowledge thrives by exercise, as well as our limbs and complexion. Truth is compared in Scripture to a streaming fountain; if her waters flow not in a perpetual progression, they sicken into a muddy pool of conformity and tradition. A man may be a heretic in the truth; and if he believe things only because his pastor says so, or the Assembly so determines, without knowing other reason, though his belief be true, yet the very truth he holds becomes his heresy.

In other words, the power of truth lies not in abstract proposi-tions but in the understanding and willful application of truth by living, breathing persons which can occur only in the context of liberty.

Indeed, for Milton, this necessary freedom is seen in the char-acter of God. For God is not, Milton argues, one to "captivate" his children "under a perpetual childhood of prescription," but rather, God expects us to exercise reason, wisdom, and virtue. "What wisdom can there be to choose . . . without knowledge of evil?" asks Milton. What praise for "a fugitive and cloistered virtue, unexercised and unbreathed, that never sallies out and sees his adversary, but slinks out of the race where that immortal garland is to be run for, not without dust and heat." Those "who imagine to remove sin by removing the matter of sin" have a poor under-standing of human nature and the human condition, argues Milton. What would Milton have said to my youth leader who burned his rock music?

And what of books, my beloved books? The "best books," Milton argues, "to a naughty mind are not unappliable to occa-sions of evil." On the other hand, "bad books," Milton continues, "to a discreet and judicious reader serve in many respects to discover, to confute, to forewarn, to illustrate." How aptly an anal-ogy might be drawn between the way Milton depicts God demanding of his children the exercise of reason, wisdom, and virtue and parents who might draw out the same in their children through liberal reading and testing of ideas through books.

But beyond the practical uses of truth in exercising virtue and cultivating maturity, Milton waxes most eloquent when he describes the very nature of truth itself:

> For who knows not that Truth is strong, next to the Almighty? She needs no policies, nor stratagems, nor licens-ings to make her victorious; those are the shifts and the defences that error uses against her power. Give her but room, and do not bind her when she sleeps . . . And though all the winds of doctrine were let loose to play upon the earth, so Truth be in the field, we do injuriously,

by licensing and prohibiting, to misdoubt her strength. Let her and Falsehood grapple; who ever knew Truth put to the worse, in a free and open encounter? Her confuting is the best and surest suppressing.

The only other passage in all of English letters that gives me goose-bumps to compete with this passage from Milton is Martin Luther King, Jr.'s "I Have a Dream" speech. Incidentally, the two works, in their most powerful moments, draw upon some of the very same scriptures.

I know that we live in an age in which many no longer believe in "Truth-with-a-capital-T," but I happen to be one who, despite being familiar with the arguments about there might not be such a thing, still believes in truth and its power. There is perhaps no better evidence to me of the power of Truth than what I read one day in a note to me from this professor who had introduced me to Milton's *Areopagitica*. He'd long left my university and his wife, and gone with a new wife to a new university in New York City. The brief message said he wasn't quite sure how it had happened—but that he had come to believe in the God of Milton's *Areopagitica*—and my God.

So this was my introduction to *Areopagitica* and, more importantly, the idea that the God I had been raised to believe in was not a God of record burning and book blotting, but a God of freedom. "You will know the truth, and the truth will set you free." I had heard this my whole life. Now I saw it to be so.

And I felt utterly liberated.

I was beginning, finally, to understand that the antagonism I had always felt between the life of the church and the life of the mind was false. Why had this truth been obscured from me for so long? Why had it seemed hidden from me by the church, only to be uncovered by an unbelieving professor? I'm not clear about where the perception of this antagonism came from—from culture, from politics, from bad preaching, or from all of the above. But the fact was that there was no essential conflict between the tenets of my faith and freedom of the mind. The oppression I had felt in the church was of human origin, not divine.

I don't want to be presumptuous in guessing how Milton might respond to current debates over controversial media and the banning of books, issues that go well beyond the doctrinal debates lurking in the background of *Areopagitica*. But I do suspect that Milton's reaction to modern day anxieties over the likes of Harry Potter and *Twilight* might be something along the lines of a deep, resigned sigh. Harry Potter and Bella the vampire lover came along well after my time, but in my day we had Stephen King, and he has to be at least as bad as J. K. Rowling and Stephanie Meyer, what with all his blood-soaked, blood-soaking teenage girls and their raving, Bible-quoting fundamentalist mothers; his decomposed pets coming back to life; his quaint, vampire-infested New England towns; and his evil-spirit possessed hotels, St. Bernards, cell phones, spacecrafts, and balloon-brandishing clowns. Stephen King's novels and the like constituted the staple of my reading through my high school years. Indeed, it is largely because of those books that the love of reading cultivated by my mother in my early years didn't dissipate, as it so often does once adolescence comes along and replaces the thrills of reading with other forms of thrill-making.

So it was King and my mother, perhaps, and a newly-imparted lesson from my professor and John Milton that drew me, so many years later, back to that place, one important stop on my journey with books: The library at Cumston Hall.

Standing there, surrounded by the smell of polished wood and musty books, I slipped my index finger into the cradle formed atop the bound pages of the book and deftly pulled *King of the Wind* from the shelf. Instinctively, I opened the inside back cover. By this time, computers had long since replaced the old-fashioned means of checking out books—signing the card, stamping a due date, and filing the card away until the book's return—so I didn't really expect to see the small sheet of lined cardstock nestled within a paper sleeve glued to the back page. Nor did I expect when I pulled the card out, after all this time, to see my own name there from so long ago. But there it was: *Karen Swallow*, printed in the large, round letters of my childhood self. My name had literally been carried inside the book for these many years. The greater truth is that I have carried this book and many, many others, all these years. And they have made me who I am.

2

The Life-Giving Power of Words: *Charlotte's Web*

Lara walked along the tracks following a path
worn by pilgrims and then turned into the fields.
Here she stopped and, closing her eyes, took a
deep breath of the flower-scented air of the
broad expanse around her. It was dearer to her
than her kin, better than a lover, wiser than a
book. For a moment she rediscovered the purpose of her life. She was here on earth to grasp
the meaning of its wild enchantment and to call
each thing by its right name.

—from Boris Pasternak, *Doctor Zhivago*

"A horse! A horse!" I shrieked and ran from the barn to find my
mother, who had chosen some less important place to be than the
barn. She followed me back to the place where I'd first run, upon
my family's arrival at my grandparents' farm.

The old barn was a behemoth, a cavernous and yawning black
space broken only by layers of wooden haylofts on one side and,
on the other, a long wall of feed troughs. Wood slats nailed in
assorted arrangements to walls and posts fashioned rough ladders
for climbing from loft to loft. Although forbidden most of the
time from doing so—such decrees made more out of concern for
nutrients in the hay than for the safety of the children—we loved
climbing up and along the beams and jumping back down into
heaps of prickly fresh-cut hay. A small milk room cornered the
left front of the building, where my grandmother separated the
cream from the smooth, warm liquid just squeezed from soft
udders. She'd pour the froth into a large, wooden barrel and churn

it with her strong hands into the best butter I've ever tasted. Everything in the barn, except the hay and the cows, was made of wood, grayish-brown splintery wood as ancient as the forests that ringed the pasture, in the midst of which the barn sat brooding.

On this mid-summer day, my family and I had arrived to pick up my brother, who'd come a week earlier to visit. My brothers and cousins and I loved my grandparents' farm, full as it was of discovery and adventure—playing in the barn, riding on the tractor, wading in the creek, fishing in the pond, building mudslides in the gravel pit, and catching frogs in the frog pond, which was really the upturned rooftop of an old school bus discovered along the grassy, upper woods trail, filled with rainwater and, in the right season, the shiny green creatures. So intrinsic to this place was the identity of my mother's parents that for years I never even knew their real surname; we had always just called them "Gramma and Grampa On-the-Farm."

Naturally, the first place I had run after jumping out of the car was the barn. I could already smell the fresh hay from June's first cutting piled loose and high in the lofts within; baling the hay required equipment my grandparents couldn't afford. I slowed upon entering the darkness. No small part of the barn's appeal was its scariness. I stuck my head through the first of the trough-mouths to peer along a row of tan-colored cow rumps whose tails swished almost in time to the chewing being done by the other end. As my gaze moved down the line of backsides, one caught my eye. It wasn't tan like the hides of the Jersey cows but black and white. Even more importantly, the tail was not the long, slender tufted stick of a cow. Instead it was covered entirely with long strands of black and white hair—horse hair!

Lacking confidence in my tail-identification skills, my mother returned with me, thinking it smartest to espy the alleged equine beast from the front. We walked down the wall of troughs, examining each moist brown bovine nose until we came, at last, to a lovely, long, whiskered, black and white horse face.

I jumped ecstatically. "See! A horse!" I exclaimed, as before. "I told you!"

And so it was. Although not quite.

The horse was actually a pony, a rather small one, but just the right size for me. It had been years since my grandparents kept horses, not since the work horses of days gone by had been replaced by tractors, making the outdated animals a luxury, the sort my grandparents, who were poorer than poor—my grandfather called it "hard up," not "poor"—could ill afford. Everything on their farm, minus the menagerie of flowers and plants my grand-mother lovingly cultivated in her little hothouse, was raised for eating or selling. The pony, as it turned out, my grandparents had rented from a local horse trader for the week of my brother's visit. Not surprisingly the weeklong rental turned into a permanent stay likely based on some fetching barter. I don't know what my brother called the pony during the preceding days, if anything, but in honor of his black and white splotches the color of Oreos I bestowed him with the name Cookie. And Cookie he was from that day forward.

Along with the love of books, the love of horses has shaped my life from my earliest years. I wasn't much more than a toddler when I first walked down the long corridor of a stable near my home, where I stared up at the delicate, beautiful faces gazing down at me through thick eyelashes, a hazy memory to be sure, but one I've never forgotten. From that moment on, I wanted to see, smell, and touch these creatures every chance I could get.

The mere love of horses, however, is a far cry from the skills required to actually ride one or care for one. I had no such skills. Nor did Cookie, like most stubborn Shetlands, have any desire to be ridden.

Nevertheless, with none of the adults equipped to give me much help, I figured out a way to ride that pony that summer on the farm. I would saddle him up the best I could and lead him by the halter from the barn down the road several hundred yards to the front steps of my grandparents' house. Then I would stand on the middle step, throw one leg over the saddle, plant myself in the seat, and hold onto the saddle horn as Cookie trotted speedily up the road back to the barn, the only place he would go of his own volition. Once there at the barn, I would repeat the process over and over: leading Cookie back to the house, lurching into the saddle, hanging on for dear life all the way back to the barn, utterly exhilarated. I was riding a horse!

Once our visit with Gramma and Grampa On-the-Farm was over, I had to leave my beloved Cookie and return to the city of Buffalo, where my family was in the midst of a three-year-stay. Upon entering my new second grade classroom that fall, I announced to everyone that I had a boyfriend back in Maine, and his name was Cookie.

Is it any wonder, then, that when I read *Charlotte's Web*, Wilbur the pig's final home with Farmer Zuckerman looked to my mind exactly like Gramma and Grampa On-the-Farm's big barn? Or that the home of Fern Arable, the main character and Wilbur's first "mother," was a lot like the small farm home my family moved back to in Maine, just twelve miles from my grandparents' farm? Fern Arable's life was, as a matter of fact, a lot like mine. Fern lived on a small farm like I did. She had an uncle who had a larger, working farm more like that of my grandparents. Fern also loved animals the way I did and talked to them like I did, and could hear them talk, too, like I sometimes thought I could.

In fact, E. B. White, the author of *Charlotte's Web*, had lived in Maine, too. Although the setting of the story is never identified, for anyone who has lived there, Maine is clearly the backdrop. In Maine, as in the book, spring comes before the snow melts. The summer is short. And the County Fair is the pinnacle of the agricultural year. This is exactly how I remember my life in Maine even decades after White published his book.

My love of animals, just like my tendency to cause alarm with sudden gasps over small matters, was inherited from my mother and from her mother before her. Our home always housed at least a dog and a cat and, over the years, sundry gerbils and guinea pigs, fish, a turtle, mice, one short-lived parakeet (see "cat," above), rabbits, and eventually—on the little farm—chickens, sheep, goats, and horses. When I was very little, I dressed my guinea pigs in my dolls' clothes and pushed them around in a toy baby carriage. We also had a sturdy little Boston Terrier named Lucky who could pull me around the floor on a towel with his strong tugging. Having all my life had animals who, whether they slept on the bed or in the barn, were considered part of the family, I've always lamented the particular poverty of children raised without pets. Learning responsibility by taking care of these fellow members of the created order was one of my parents' many gifts to me. I've no doubt that the greatest richness of a deeply rich childhood came— along with the love of my parents and the love of books—from the love of animals. These three things are so intertwined that it is difficult, if not impossible, for me to separate for very long, any single thread in the tapestry of my childhood.

Such love for animals, and a knowledge of the sometimes harsh realities of farm life, made me a ready reader of *Charlotte's Web*. I easily identified with eight-year-old Fern. She put two and two together pretty quickly when she saw that her father was headed out to the hog house with an ax to "do away with" the runt of a litter born the night before. I understood Fern's desire to save the piglet's life despite knowing, as she also knew, that the pig had been bred and born for eventual slaughter. Even so, I rejoiced with Fern at her father's reluctant relent to Fern's cries: the life of the runt would be spared and placed under Fern's care. No matter that Mr. Arable sought to teach Fern a lesson about the effort required to care for a runt. Fern's mother seemed to understand, though. A good mother, Mrs. Arable helped Fern to mother the little runt named Wilbur.

My own mother helped me to fill a similar role. Every spring on our little farm, we purchased a clutch of unhatched eggs with little chicks inside. We placed them under bright lights to keep them warm until it was time for them to break free from their shells. One year, a chick didn't hatch out of his shell with the rest of his clan. We could hear him peeping weakly from within, but for whatever reason he couldn't muster the strength to make his way out. So my mother affixed a hot bulb above a cardboard box which she set on the kitchen counter with the unhatched egg placed gently inside. When I gingerly held the translucent egg up to the light, I could see the outline of a rough, squirming mass inside, and I could hear faint tapping from inside the delicate orb. When I peeped at the egg, the dark shape inside peeped back. My mother made a tiny hole in the egg and showed me how to break away a small segment of the egg every hour or so.

The chick kept tapping. Little by little, hour by hour, I broke off fragments of shell. The entire time, I kept peeping at the chick and he peeped back at me. When the chick was at last fully free, I was the first thing he saw. And quick as that, I was his mother. I named him Peeper.

Even when Peeper was full grown and had made his home in the chicken coop with the rest of the chickens, he would fly to me and sit on my shoulder whenever I entered the coop. Of course, I knew all along that Peeper, like the rest of the young roosters, had come to us to be food for our family. I don't remember how long I imagined he might escape that fate, but eventually of course, he outgrew his chick-ness. When the time came to slaughter his peers, he had become like them: mean and surly, no longer treating me like his mother. When, along with the rest of his brethren, his neck was placed under an ax like the one Fern caught her father carrying to the hog house and he took his place with the others in our freezer, I did not grieve. Not much. This was life on a farm.

Yet, even while accepting the harsh facts of life, I still harbored, like Fern, the kind of love for animals some might describe as sentimental. Tempered as that love was and is today with an honestly-gained knowledge of the natural order, I think it is better described as an attitude of respect. Respect for all creatures, respect for the order of creation, for the chain of being and the knowledge that as merely one link on the chain, my life depends on the lives of so many others, and that while the chains might be made of steel, they are linked most strongly by love.

Neither sentimentality nor human love can overturn the order of nature, except perhaps temporarily. When we assist nature in bringing animals into the world, we take on a responsibility whose magnitude is easy to ignore. When we help create a life—even the life of some small insignificant creature destined for the dinner plate or a life of servitude to humankind—we become a handmaiden to Mother Nature. So in saving Wilbur's life, Fern becomes a sort of mother to him, by giving back the life he came so close to losing as a newborn. When I was the same age as Fern, I also took on this creative, mothering role in bringing into being some of these dependent creatures, one even more involved than that of helping to hatch Peeper from his shell.

It began with a handsome male rabbit named Buster. He was pure white except for black-tipped ears and a stark black ring around each eye. Every year I entered him in the Monmouth Fair, proud of how fine he looked. And every year, without fail, regardless of the other rabbits that happened to be throwing their hats into the ring, Buster—like Wilbur in Charlotte's Web—came home with the red second-place ribbon. He never got the blue, not even once. But no matter. Blue ribbon or no, Buster was gainfully and happily employed back home making little bunnies with Ebony (of obvious color) and Annie, a large, gray rabbit, who had been lucky enough to bring home a blue ribbon. When each litter of bunnies Buster and the girls produced was old enough, I would put them in a cardboard box, ride with them in the car to the pet store in the city, and pocket a little bit of money, feeling a little more independent than I would have had I taken all the expenses of this venture into account.

One day, my rabbit-breeding business made me grow up far beyond what pocket change could ever accomplish. I walked into the barn, opened Ebony's hutch to feed and water her, and saw the mutilated remains of tiny newborn rabbits strewn throughout her cage. I hadn't even known she was expecting a litter. I ran to my mother, traumatized. She explained to me that sometimes animals do such things if something has gone wrong with either mother or the babies.

I was horrified. Mother Nature could be a cruel parent. I never wanted to be responsible for such destruction again. I retired from the rabbit breeding business for good. And so did Buster, Annie, and Ebony. Little did I know that a similar but even harder lesson was yet to come. While the sentiments of Charlotte's Web remained real for me, the happy outcome of the story would prove to be the phantasm of mere fiction.

When I was eleven, all of my dreams came true: my parents bought me a horse. Neither Mom nor Dad knew anything about horses, but they got enough advice from those more knowledgeable to find me a nice little Morgan mare named El Diablo. Mom didn't like the idea of calling a horse "devil," not even in Spanish, so we called her by her nickname, Dabs. A neighbor of ours had a young Morgan stallion he was anxious to put to stud, so he and my parents agreed to try out his horse on my mare, at no cost to us.

I couldn't believe that my first horse would so quickly multiply to two! Once we knew Dabs was in foal, I counted every day until the expected birth the next summer. After wanting a horse my whole life, not only did I have one, but by the next year, I would have my own foal to raise, too, just like the kids in the countless horse books I'd read.

While Dabs was building a baby in her body, I was building character, though I didn't really know it. Having wanted a horse for so long, my parents expected—and required—that her care be my responsibility. It's not like there was much choice anyway, seeing as no one else in my family was a horse person. Even my mother, the greatest animal lover in our family besides me, was a bit afraid of these large creatures. So each morning before school, I had to get myself up to go to the barn and feed and water my horse before getting myself ready for the bus.

Maine winters, especially, made this no easy feat: without running water in the barn, I had to pull buckets of water—only three-quarters full to reduce spilling—from the house by means of a plastic sled pulled across frozen snow each morning. I would bring back buckets of the frozen-solid water remaining from the previous evening and place them by the woodstove to melt in time for the next feeding when the cycle would be repeated. Having a well that had once gone dry meant that no drop of water should be wasted. I had a quirky black and white cat named Oscar—with my Maine accent, I pronounced his name "Aw-ska"—that had come from a litter born on my grandparents' farm and, Oscar, unlike my two other cats, was my faithful companion on these treks to the barn and back. Sometimes Oscar would ride on the sled with the water buckets and other times he'd lie across my shoulders and the back of my neck, a living, purring fur stole. How could I have complained about such work, labor, as it was, of love?

Perhaps my memory is too generous toward myself, but I don't recall ever complaining. I had wanted a horse for nearly my whole life, and at last I had one.

Those eleven months of waiting for the foal to arrive were torturously long.

I was still in bed early one late summer morning when my oldest brother hollered up the stairs from the kitchen. "Karen, you better get down here quick!" I knew from the excitement in his voice what had happened. I squealed and leaped out of bed, ran down the stairs, out the front door and through the pasture gate, still in my light flannel nightgown. I ran and ran through the field, looking for Dabs until I spotted her on the crest of the hill near the back fence line, calmly cropping the tender, early grass, as though this were just a normal morning. The sun was still low in the sky behind her, making the mare glow. I slowed to a gentle walk and approached softly. I couldn't see the foal at first, but then, there, lying flat in the tall grass, warming in the sun, I saw a tiny bush of a tail flicking back and forth.

Quietly, so as not to disturb him or alarm his mother, I eased closer and sat down on the ground, cross-legged, beside the colt, pulling my nightgown across my knees. He lifted his head slightly. When he put it down again, it was in my lap, resting on the sling my nightgown made as it stretched across my legs. The colt was still sticky from being inside his mother's body and then washed by her tongue; a few flies flocked to the dried liquid around his eyes. How long I sat there with the newborn's head in my lap, gently brushing the flies away while his mother grazed warily, but contentedly, beside us, I don't know. But it felt like a glorious eternity. The world was still except for the sun rising silently above us.

It was, as I said, a boy, a son of Dabs and, in my childish way of thinking, a son of mine. Once again, I tapped into that same power God gave to Adam in Genesis when God instructed the first man to name the animals, and the same power Charlotte exerted when she wove in her web magical words about Wilbur. I named my colt Sonny Boy.

But colts, especially those belonging to young girls unskilled in horse training, grow into stubborn stallions who don't take kindly to being told what to do. Even after being gelded, Sonny was, I reluctantly allowed myself to admit, more than I could handle. Dabs was quite a handful, too, as a matter of fact. I painfully realized and my parents agreed that I needed a well-trained horse and some lessons myself if I were ever going to do more than ride around in the pasture wherever Dabs decided to take me. With careful effort, I found Dabs a good home with a girl about my age who lived a couple of hours away in a coastal town in eastern Maine. The girl wrote to me and sent pictures, and my parents even drove me there to visit so I could see Dabs happily settled in her new home.

As for Sonny, well, a young untrained colt is a harder sell. A horse trader down the road from us had said since Sonny was born he was a fine-looking horse, and to let him know if I ever wanted to sell him. But I wasn't going to let Sonny go to a dealer in horseflesh who'd sell him off to God knows where for mere profit. I'd read about that sort in plenty of horse books. I wanted to ensure myself that Sonny went to a good home.

When a young, newly-married woman who wanted a competition horse answered my ad and showed up at our door to look at Sonny, I judged her as suitable. She was a little bit rough around the edges, but I'd already learned that lots of horse people were. We made an agreement, and week or so later the woman and her husband came with a rented trailer—not a horse trailer but a U-Haul—to take Sonny to his new home. I had held a long tearful good-bye to my baby boy the night before, so I took comfort in my promise to visit Sonny in his new home.

A few months later, I did. I was surprised when we arrived to find that the woman lived in a trailer park and that Sonny's new home was a small grass lot at the end of it. It made me remember the improper sort of trailer they'd picked him up in. I was disappointed, too, that his new owner had changed his name to Sonny Blue Boy—and she called him Blue Boy, not Sonny, for short. I was anxious when we went to watch a show she'd entered him in for just how hard Sonny was being ridden in the barrel racing competition. He was only two, too early to ride a young horse so hard, even though lots of people did so.

One more thing I'd read about in my horse stories.

I was doubtful, but I also knew I was not very knowledgeable in these things, so I pushed the nagging questions away. I could see his new owner loved Sonny. And he looked so regal in the pictures she sent me after our visit, decked out in his Western show gear, a blue ribbon hanging from his bridle. I was proud of this wonderful creature I'd brought into the world.

I didn't worry when I stopped hearing from Sonny's new owner. Life goes on. I had a new horse. This time my parents had enlisted some expert help in buying a horse as well as in riding lessons for me. This horse was highly trained and easy to ride. She had been born on Presidents' Day, a holiday that still meant a day off from school in those New England days, so she had been named Freedom. The girl I bought her from called her Fred for short, but I couldn't bring myself to do so. I thought Freedom was a beautiful and perfect name, and finally, once I learned from my lessons the rules of riding and horsemanship, I was able to experience the real freedom of true horsemanship.

I began competing in horse shows and winning some, too. Yet I never felt freer than when Freedom and I roamed the countryside, and I galloped her bareback across dirt roads. I had come a long way since the days of trotting Cookie up and down the road at my grandparents' farm. I knew it and embraced it.

About two years after selling Sonny, I received a call from our neighbor, the horse trader, to whom I'd so proudly refused to sell Sonny. "I just picked up a horse that I want you to come and see," he said. "I think it's your colt."

"Sonny?" I asked, confused. How in the world would Sonny have ended up back down the road from me after all this time?

"I think it's him," the trader said, "but I'm not sure." His voice grew softer. "I can't tell, really. You need to come and look at him." He paused. "I need to warn you. He don't look good."

I went right away. The horse dealer was just around the corner, less than a mile away, just past the old, overgrown graveyard where my cousins and I used to play. It was not much past five o'clock, but it was winter, when night falls early in Maine. I walked into the dark, cramped barn where horses were tied up like cows rather than given their own stalls. This was why I hadn't wanted Sonny to come here in the first place.

"Here he is," the horse trader said, cautiously. I had never had this much interaction with the man. His kindness took me aback. I had never thought of a horse trader as being kind. I had read about plenty of them in books, and they were always greedy and cruel.

His caution could not have prepared me for what I saw, however. The creature standing in front of me was mere bones cloaked by dull brown hair. He was not tied up because there was no need to do so. His head hung low, and his cloudy eyes stared off into the distance, as if to some other time or place. As bad as all this was, the worst was the horse's legs—they were bent and deformed, bowed as though he could barely hold up even the slight weight of his emaciated body. I didn't recognize him without the high, proud carriage of his neck and head for which the Morgan breed is so well-known, and without the shiny bay coat that had emerged out from under that soft down I had stroked long ago that summer morning of his birth.

The horse dealer said something about buying him at a horse auction from a lady going through a divorce, but he didn't know much more than that. I prayed it wasn't Sonny. I wasn't sure if I could be sure either way. Perhaps it would be better not to really know. But then I saw something on the blue nylon halter that hung loosely around his head. Someone had written in black marker on the halter.

I got closer. Sonny Blue Boy, it said.

"Is this the halter he had on when you got him?" I asked the trader.

"Ayuh. That's the one he come with."

"It's him. It's Sonny," I said. I placed my face gently against his dirty, matted neck and christened him with my tears.

A few days later, the horse trader told me, in his gentle, gruff way, that there was nothing to be done; the damage was too great. "His legs were just too bad. He couldn't stand anymore." Mercifully, he had put Sonny down.

I knew that ultimately this was my doing. I had brought this horse into the world, and I had failed him in the worst possible way that a living creature can be failed. I wore—and still wear—the weight of this responsibility. I never again brought an animal into the world.

Yes, Mother Nature herself, unassisted by human beings, populates the planet with, at present, 1.7 million (more or less) animal species. Who knows how many in ages past and to come? Perhaps a young girl's shouldering the weight of the sad fate of just one of these creatures is an unnecessary, sentimental burden. Perhaps that girl felt a bit too deeply. Yet, Jesus said that not even one sparrow falls to the ground outside of God's care. I believe in a God who knew about Sonny, too. And that means He also knew about this one girl and the way she failed Sonny. I'm not sure why I find that comforting. Some might not, but I do.

In rescuing Wilbur from her father's ax, Fern takes on no small responsibility. In saving Wilbur's life she becomes, in effect, his second mother. Fern's mother, like my mother once did for Peeper, lets the kitchen become a nursery for the runt. Fern bottle feeds Wilbur in her arms while sitting on the kitchen floor. She pushes him about in her doll's carriage, as I had once done with my guinea pigs, and when he outgrows the cardboard box in the kitchen, she feeds and plays with him each day in his small yard under the apple tree. But when Wilbur grows past piglethood, he is sold to Fern's Uncle Homer, who lives down the road. Uncle Homer raises pigs not for pets but for meat. It would seem that Fern's intervention on behalf of the runt will merely delay an inevitable doom, just as it did for my rooster Peeper.

But then the unlikeliest of heroines—a spider—enters the picture. In Wilbur's new home in the manure pile at Uncle Homer's barn, which, again, in my mind's eye looks exactly like the barn of my Gramma and Grampa On-the-Farm, he meets someone he finds at first rather frightening and gruesome. After all, as Wilbur discovers, she eats flies. Not only that, the spider boasts, but she also eats "grasshoppers, choice beetles, moths, butterflies, centipedes, mosquitoes, crickets—anything careless enough to get caught in my web." Wilbur can barely stand it when the spider further explains, "I don't really eat them. I drink them—drink their blood." When Wilbur protests and says he doesn't want to hear any more, she asks, "Why not? It's true, and I have to say what is true. I am not entirely happy about my diet of flies and bugs, but it's the way I'm made." Mother Nature, once again. "In good time," however, Wilbur learns "that he was mistaken about Charlotte" for she "prove[s] loyal and true to the very end."

Wilbur's first hint about Charlotte's true character comes when she tells him her name, Charlotte A. Cavatica. What an oddly beautiful name for a creature usually associated with ugliness, fear, and death. Upon hearing her name, Wilbur tells Charlotte, "I think you're beautiful." And Charlotte, naturally, agrees.

Names are powerful words. We don't think about names quite the same way people of old did, and this is our great error. In ancient times, a person's name often signified an event, a personal quality, or a family relation. In this way, a name offered not only a label for oneself, but even more importantly, a connection to the world one was born into and a part of. The acts of naming and being named were momentous events laden with significance— just as it is significant that the first work God gave Adam in the Garden of Eden was naming the animals. To name something or someone is a gesture that is both creative and powerful. In *Charlotte's Web*, E. B. White bestowed a spider with the name of Charlotte A. Cavatica. And he gave a little girl—just like me—the name of Fern Arable, a name resonant with the pastoral qualities that permeate the pages of the book.

As for me, my mother chose my middle name, Irene, first because it is my grandmother's name, and then she picked a first name suitable to accompany it. For most of my life, I thought of Irene as an old, ugly name. But now that I am older, and my grandmother is much more so, and I can better appreciate who she is and the life she has lived, I think it is a pure, strong name. Its origin is Greek; it means *peace*. I'm thankful for this name, not only because I think it is beautiful in both sound and sense, but even more because it came from my mother, and my grandmother, and it connects me to the world I was born into and became a part of.

All words are names, for all words signify something. The power of naming is a subset of the power of all language.

God spoke the universe into existence and, in giving us the gift of language He gave us a lesser, but still magnificent, creative power in the ability to name: the power to communicate, to make order out of chaos, to tell stories, and to shape our own lives and the lives of others.

The Book of Proverbs says that death and life are in the power of words. To choose a good word, to assign the right name, to arrange proper words in the best order: these are no easy tasks. Such work requires the creative power, the brooding, the birth pangs of a mother. Names, words, and language: they shape and create our souls the way a mother's body shapes and creates our bodies. We describe the country of our origin as our fatherland, but our language we call our mother tongue. Indeed the words that often wield the greatest power in and over our lives are those spoken by our mothers, from our names, to words of encouragement, to words that define and shape our character, words of truth spoken in love. This power of words is akin to the creative, nurturing role a mother plays in our lives.

The getting of meaning, like the getting of a child, is an act of nature and grace. Yet, it's an act so every day, so commonplace that we easily overlook its magnitude. Until we see that same power in a new and surprising context, exerted, for example, by a fictional spider on behalf of a fictional pig.

Charlotte's Web is a metaphor for the power words have to shape us into who others see us as well as how we see ourselves. For it is through words that Charlotte saves Wilbur's life—not temporarily, as Fern has, but forever, at least the sort of forever that's contained within the pages of a book. By knitting those words into her web which stretches above Wilbur's pigpen, Charlotte makes the pig the talk of the town. No one, not even a farmer like Homer Zuckerman whose livelihood depends upon the fruit of his toiling, does away with a pig as special as Wilbur, one who gains widespread fame and visitors from near and far. Even when Wilbur loses first place at the County Fair to a much bigger pig, Wilbur's life is no less secure than was my rabbit's for his award of the red ribbon each year at the Monmouth Fair. Yet, Charlotte's words not only save Wilbur's life, they shape his life.

As she weaves words about Wilbur into her web, Wilbur tries to live up to the meaning of the words. "Some pig," she proclaims. "Terrific," she writes. And as if by magic, Charlotte's serendipitously chosen words create in everyone who comes to see Wilbur, and even in Wilbur himself, a sense of being, in fact, "some pig," and a pretty "terrific" one, too.

Wilbur protests when Charlotte chooses the word "terrific," that he's not terrific: "That doesn't make a particle of difference," replied Charlotte. "Not a particle. People believe almost anything they see in print." When she chooses the word "radiant," she puts Wilbur through a series of tests to see if he is. And Wilbur does "everything possible to make himself glow."

Charlotte observes critically: "I'm not sure Wilbur's action is exactly radiant, but it's interesting."

"Actually," said Wilbur. "I feel radiant."

And the last word that Charlotte makes for Wilbur, "humble," foretells both his second place ribbon and the ordinary but happy natural life her words allow him to live out.

When I was a child, I overheard my mother talking to some other adults. I was only half-attentive until I heard my mother speak my name. "Karen's very perceptive," my mother was telling them.

I piped up: "What does that mean? *Perceptive?*"

My mother hesitated, searching for another word. "Deep," she finally explained. I wasn't entirely sure what she meant by that either, but I do remember understanding that somehow, in some way, my mother noticed something that distinguished me, something she could name even if I could not. From that moment and for the rest of my life, my mother's words—perceptive and many others—have helped me to be the thing she saw and named in me.

Like the old riddle of the chicken and the egg, the power of giving something its proper name, in turn, empowers it to become the name it is called; which comes first matters little, perhaps. My mother's word for me foretold the anguish I would feel when that living creature I helped bring into the world and gave a name, Sonny Boy, gave up his life because of my faltering. But depth runs in both directions: one who feels anguish deeply can live life deeply, too, and strive to help others do the same. The length of life is decreed by nature, its depth by grace.

Charlotte, through her words, gives Wilbur life, just as her own life is nearing an end, but her life-giving role is not over yet. She leaves behind dozens of offspring, born in Wilbur's barnyard under his watchful eye. Three of these stay on in Zuckerman's barn to be Wilbur's companions, though none can replace Charlotte, for as the narrator says, "It's not often that someone comes along who is a true friend and a good writer. Charlotte was both."

Like a true friend and a good writer, right words are hard to find. And all of these, like a mother, have the power to give life.

3

God of the Awkward, the Freckled, and the Strange: Gerard Manley Hopkins's "Pied Beauty"

> He plunged under once and this time, the waiting current caught him like a long gentle hand and pulled him swiftly forward and down. For an instant he was overcome with surprise: then since he was moving quickly and knew that he was getting somewhere, all his fury and fear left him.
>
> —from Flannery O'Connor, "The River"

"Come here. I want to tell you something," Mickey said, beckoning me with one curled finger. Steam covered the lenses of her crooked glasses, from her breath caught by the snorkel jacket's furry hood tied close around her face.

I had just told her it was time for me to go, and I didn't want to linger. My toes ached as they always did when I stayed playing outside for too long on cold winter days. In Maine, cold means below freezing, often closer to zero, even during the day. This was a snow day and we were off from school. We'd had a blast digging tunnels into snow drifts higher than the tallest of us kids and burrowing in and out of them for hours. Shivering, I sighed, stepped toward Mickey and leaned the side of my face toward hers, flushed pink with cold, in order to hear her secret.

She leaned closer and planted two wet, awkward lips on my cheek. I froze, but only for a split-second.

"I've got to go now," I said, as coolly as I could. I turned and trotted off toward home, a quarter-mile away. As I neared my house, I ran faster and faster, putting as much distance as I could between me and that kiss I never told anyone about.

Mickey Cotter—her real name was Michelle, but everyone called her Mickey—and I were eleven, too young to have kissed any boys, but old enough to know that girls weren't supposed to kiss each other. Mickey, however, wasn't a regular girl. She was what people our parents' age called "a tomboy," but that wasn't it either. Mickey looked like a boy. Acted like a boy. And now she'd tried to kiss me, like a boy. Had kissed me, actually, I realized as I wiped the spot with my hand as soon as I was out of Mickey's sight. My cheek began to chafe in the cold wind that whipped against me all the way home.

I still went over to Mickey's to play after that day. There were cows to ride, woods to play in, and a tree fort to sleep in, after all. But the next time she told me she wanted to whisper something to me, I just shook my head. She never asked again.

It wasn't really my idea to play with Mickey and her five brothers and sisters. My family lived three miles outside of town, and there weren't any other kids nearby, but I'd have been happy to play by myself with my animals if it weren't for my parents who always made me be nice, especially to people like the Cotters.

My mom picked up stray kids like some people pick up stray puppies. She was always finding some kid or two, or a whole flock of them, whose parents didn't go to church but who agreed to letting us pick their kids up on Sundays, or every day during the week of Vacation Bible School, to go to church with us. There were Maggie and Billy, who lived in a big old house that had gone completely gray for lack of paint, and had two big brothers who were all grown and gone, and whose parents looked older than my grandparents; there was the youngest Chamberlain boy, whom we picked up way down a dirt road at a house sitting in a yard strewn with rusted farm equipment, old cars, empty paint buckets, ratty-looking cats, and a stray chicken or two; and, then of course, there were the Cotters.

Until the oldest of the La Croix sons built a log cabin in the cow pasture across the road, the Cotters were our closest neighbors. All eight of them lived in a trailer planted next to Old Mr. Cotter's, the grandfather's, rundown farm house. The three girls shared one bedroom in the trailer, and the three boys another bedroom. The kids wrote on the dark faux-paneled walls of their rooms with crayons and markers, something my parents would never have let me do, and I politely declined joining in when invited to do so. Mrs. Cotter was a squat woman with dark hair and skin who sat at the table of the kitchenette all day smoking cigarettes and alternating cackling laughter with sudden screeches directed in alternating shifts at each of the kids for some misbehavior or another. Half of the Cotter kids had her dark features and the other half had flaming red hair and freckles like Mr. Cotter. I always thought I had a lot of freckles until I met the Cotter kids.

Cotter kids or no, I did have a lot of freckles. And I didn't like them one bit. I didn't like those or my big front teeth or my large, protruding eyes that inspired a boy in my class, Derrick, to call me "fish eyes" one day. Derrick was the first kid in our class whose parents got divorced. That seemed to me like a great deal more trouble than I had, even with my freckles, big teeth, and fish eyes, so I forgave him for calling me that, even though he didn't ask me to. Besides, at least I wasn't fat like Mrs. Cotter and one of Mickey's sisters, the older one, Roberta. Or so I thought.

Until one mid-summer day, when the *Sears Back-to-School Catalog* arrived in the mail.

I loved summer, but I loved going back to school, too. I especially loved getting new school clothes each fall. So I flipped through the new catalog gazing lovingly at each page in the Junior Miss section, playing my regular game of picking out the one thing—just one!—on each page that I liked best. This summer, when I got to the end of the Junior Miss section, I saw another section that I'd never seen before. It was called "Pretty Plus." I wasn't sure what this was, but the clothes looked similar to those I'd seen on the previous pages, if plainer, so I continued looking. The section had only three or four pages, but by the time I got to the end of it, my heart had dropped into my belly. These were clothes for girls my age—but girls of a bigger size. And the more I looked at the models, the more I could not deny what I had recognized right away but didn't want to see: they looked like me. Yes, I was

"Pretty Plus," and I was overwhelmed with a sense of shame I'd never felt before.

My brother had always called me fat, but he was mean and stupid, so I had never believed him. I had regular arms and regular legs. But I was short and just a little thick in the middle. In a few years, I would learn from fashion magazines that I had what was called an "apple shape." It was the shape of my mother and my grandmother and my great grandmother, too, whom I could barely remember. I had never seen myself as fat, but here was an authority on these things—the Sears catalog, maker of the annual Christmas Wishbook—pinpointing me as "Pretty Plus." I could not deny it. The proof was in the pictures.

That was the year I started writing poetry.

Most of the poetry, maybe all of it, was about horses. Most of it, maybe all of it, was pretty bad.

But maybe one poem was good. It was good enough for a young man who came home once with my brother on their break from logging school—who happened to be a singer-songwriter as well as a logging apprentice—to put it to music. Some months later, my parents drove me on a snowy night to a city a couple of hours away so we could hear him perform it during a concert held in a darkened, nearly empty, high school auditorium. He called me up on stage when he introduced the song, and I felt a little bit like a star—but even more conscious, standing up there, of my barrel belly and big teeth. I felt shy and proud all at once. Jason, the singer-songwriter, was cute. I knew he would never have tried to kiss me like Mickey did.

So I kept writing poetry and feeling like I had been given my toothy, apple body by mistake because I didn't feel on the inside like I looked on the outside. Writing poetry helped me feel like I could escape the limits of my uncooperative body. I wondered if Mickey felt the same way about her body, but I never asked her.

It wasn't just writing poetry that made me feel better. I liked reading poetry, too. And all kinds of books. I carried a book with me wherever I went. For all the years I was too young to stay home by myself and was dragged to my older brothers' sporting events, I read books the entire time. During summers of Little League baseball, instead of sitting on top of the blanket my mother brought for me, I lay on the grass, elbows on the ground, chin cupped in my hands, blanket thrown over me like a tent to shield my reading eyes from the glare of the sun. In winter when we sat on hard wooden bleachers inside the basketball court where my brothers played, I leaned back against the footrest above me and read and read and read while the people all around me watching the dribbling, passing, and shooting noisily stomped and clapped and cheered.

Such voracious reading was both a source of and escape from my awkwardness.

It wasn't until many years later—years after reading nursery rhymes, followed by silly limericks, then poems by Robert Frost and Edgar Allan Poe, and then Shakespeare—that I first encountered the poetry of Gerard Manley Hopkins. Hopkins' poetry is odd and beautiful; its beauty, in fact, comes from its strange words, sounds, and images. I think it's fair to say that if it weren't for Hopkins' own sense of not quite fitting in, his poetry would not be so powerful. Like mine, it might never have even been written if not for his pain.

Unlike my poetry, however, Hopkins' poetry was good. Really good. But he didn't think so. He even burned it all once. It wasn't that he thought his poetry was badly-written; it's just that he thought he shouldn't write poetry at all.

Hopkins, a convert to Roman Catholicism, fought most of his life against the body: against his body, against the body of his poetic works, and against bodily desires he didn't want to have. His body was small, delicately-featured, and often sick; he mistakenly thought that writing poetry would distract him from the spiritual life; and he felt a sexual desire for men, the indulgence of which would be contrary to the teachings of the church.

Shortly after deciding to pursue the priesthood, a refuge, perhaps, against the storm of desires, Hopkins built a bonfire for his poems. Like his passions, the poems burned and then, seemingly, were gone.

Another fire, years after the moment with Mickey, burned down the Cotters' trailer. The sirens awakened my family in early hours of the morning, and we watched helplessly from our front porch as their home burned to the ground. Mickey, wrapped in the thin cotton blanket she'd managed to drag out of the fire with her, was brought to our house to spend the night. The rest of the family went to their grandparents' next door, and that's where the family stayed from that night on.

After that, when I went over to the Cotters to play, we all sat around the big dining room table in Old Mr. and Mrs. Cotter's ramshackle house, playing card games while everyone made fun of everyone else and swore until the younger Mrs. Cotter screeched. Old Mrs. Cotter, the grandmother, didn't play cards or speak. She was mute. She just sat at the table, joining in with lively eyes. Sometimes when she laughed silently, her false teeth would slip out. She'd look around sheepishly and pop them back in and giggle to herself, and sometimes to me when I caught her eye. By the time I entered junior high, hanging out with the Cotters, especially Mickey, felt more and more uncomfortable—whether because of their poverty, the swearing and screeching, or my new friendships, or all of these reasons, I don't know. My mother stopped making me go.

Remember how in grade school, kids used to be mean to other kids by saying they had "the cooties"? In our school, instead of saying "the cooties," they said, "the Cotters." If you got too close to one of the Cotter kids (and there were a lot of them), you might get teased for having "the Cotters." Or you might just get accused of having "the Cotters" for any old, random social transgression. Since I hung out with the Cotters on my own time, and not at school, I never got teased that way. Mickey was in the lowest caste of girls in our class, so there was little danger of much interaction on the school grounds. The only time I remember seeing her at school was later, in junior high when a bunch of us were playing some kind of ball game on the front lawn and a new kid kept referring to Mickey as "he" and "him." I don't remember if anyone offered a correction.

It was the church that helped correct Hopkins' errant view that his pursuit of poetry and a religious vocation were incompatible. After burning his poems, he didn't write any more poetry for many years, but sometime after he had taken his vows of poverty, chastity, and obedience as a Jesuit priest, his religious superior asked him to write a poem to commemorate the sinking of a ship which had claimed many lives, including those of several nuns. After doing so, Hopkins began writing poetry again. Yet, the world was not permitted to see these works of beauty and would not until after his death from typhoid fever at age 48. His embrace of poetry was, sadly, awkward still. He fought his poetic desires like he fought his bodily ones. But these are not battles that are always easily won. Sometimes, perhaps, they are not battles that can be won.

In his effort to quell the call of all fleshly desires—and is not poetry, with its sounds, rhythms, and images a kind of fleshly desire?—Hopkins had resisted not only poetry but with it beauty, tied as it is, in most ways of thinking, to the physical world. But beauty—like truth and goodness—will out. Beauty is so powerful that it erupts even in the most unlikely of places. Awkward places, too.

One of Hopkins' loveliest poems is about this kind of beauty, "Pied Beauty." It goes like this:

Glory be to God for dappled things—
        For skies of couple-colour as a brinded cow;
                For rose-moles all in stipple upon trout that swim;
        Fresh-firecoal chestnut-falls; finches' wings;
                Landscape plotted and pieced—fold, fallow, and plough;
                        And áll trades, their gear and tackle and trim.
All things counter, original, spáre, strange; .
        Whatever is fickle, frecklèd (who knows how?)
                With swíft, slów; sweet, sóur; adázzle, dím;
He fathers-forth whose beauty is pást change:
                        Práise hím.

It's as impossible to paraphrase a poem as it is to paraphrase a person. But like beautiful and interesting people, beautiful and interesting poems beg examination.

Pied means *patched* or *splotchy in color*. The title is an oxymoron, for beauty is not traditionally associated with the patched or splotchy things. Or the freckled or big-bellied things. The poem is filled with words and images evoking the beauty of such—things both natural and manmade that aren't smooth, uniform, or even, the qualities traditionally associated with beauty. The poem is a celebration of the awkward things: rose-moles, pieced land, gear and tackle and trim, and brindled cows.

We once had a Boxer of brindle color, rich, honeyed brown streaked with black. A birth defect resulted in the eventual removal of her deformed front leg. We named this awkward, three-legged creature Gracie. She was strong and muscular and loved to drink water right out of the spigot. I would caress the dimpled place where her leg used to be and think about how beautiful she was in her bold asymmetry. I loved her more than I have loved any animal in the world, and more than most people. We used to take her everywhere, and everyone else loved her, too. Often, after seeing Gracie run and play with as much passion and agility as any four-legged pup, people would begin to tell us stories of disability, sometimes their own, sometimes someone else's. They would tell of an accident, or illness, or war scene, all the while scratching Gracie's ears or the scruff of her neck. They would tell of victory and overcoming and joy, too. When Gracie died from a tick borne disease when she was only six, we got a new dog right away to try to fill the hole she left in our lives, but I couldn't stop crying for her for a year.

Gracie's short, irregular life brought unexpected beauty into the world. This is what Hopkins' poem "Pied Beauty" is about. And what it is, too. Not only does its content celebrate the beauty of "all things counter" and "strange," but the form of the poem itself is irregular, from the new words Hopkins creates out of strange combinations ("fathers-forth") to his invented pattern of sound using "sprung rhythm," to the very structure of the poem. The structure mimics a sonnet, but then breaks all the rules of the form, none more dramatically than the abrupt, foreshortened end of the poem with the two sudden words of finality, "Praise him." *Praise him,* the poems asks—no, commands—for the awkward things: the fickle, the freckled, the big teeth, the three-legged dogs, the girls that act like boys, and those that are "Pretty Plus."

There is, the poem reminds us, a certain kind of beauty that arises only from imperfection—or pain.

By the time I read Hopkins' poem for the first time, I had long outgrown writing horse poems, I'd grown into my barrel belly and big teeth, and witnessed the fading of my freckles. I had become a teacher and become surer of myself. I could celebrate knowingly with the poet all things spare and strange because I had overcome feeling so myself, mostly. I had come to see that poetry was not a means of escape, but rather an art of reconciliation. For poetry is made in the discovery of resemblances. It seeks likenesses, even amidst the strangeness of differences. Perhaps this is what Hopkins knew, and feared enough to burn.

By the time I reached Junior High, I'd stopped hanging around with Mickey. She and the older of her siblings had started turning down our offers of going to Sunday school, the youngest Cotter, Eddie, still went with us from time to time. Eddie was about seven now, and I was a teenager. He was one of the red-haired, freckled Cotters who looked like his dad. One day, we had an extra full carload already and stopped to pick up the Chamberlain boy, too. "Squish together," my mother said from the driver's seat. "We need to make room for one more in the back seat."

I was sitting next to Eddie, who was in the middle. It was summer, and summer days in Maine are almost as hot as winter days are cold. My mostly bare legs were stuck to the red vinyl seat of my mom's AMC Hornet station wagon. The car door next to me was opening, and Chamberlain boy was climbing in, so I peeled my thighs off the seat as I slid over until my shoulders touched Eddie's.

"Don't get too close," he warned, looking at me seriously. "You'll get the Cotters."

He said this as matter-of-factly as he might have said his age was seven or that his hair was red or that he shared an attic room with his two brothers in his grandparents' farmhouse. His words crumpled my heart, yet I didn't know what to say. So I said nothing.

Still. I write it now—for Eddie, Mickey, and me.

4

The Magic of Story: *Great Expectations*

When there is a tendency to compartmentalize
the spiritual and make it resident in a certain type
of life only, the spiritual is apt gradually to be lost.

—Flannery O'Connor, *Mystery and
Manners: Occasional Prose*

I loved Mrs. Lovejoy.

I loved everything Mrs. Lovejoy taught me because I loved
her. Or perhaps I loved Mrs. Lovejoy because she taught English,
which I also loved.

Because I loved her, I believed in Mrs. Lovejoy, too. And because I believed in her, I believed in everything Mrs. Lovejoy
taught my seventh and eighth grade English classes. I believed in
grammar and parts of speech and sentence diagramming and
punctuation and spelling quizzes and vocabulary lists and stories.
Especially the stories.

Mrs. Lovejoy was like an interesting character in a good story.
She was as thin and tall as a birch tree, and just as silver and
smooth. She was older than dirt, too. Peering down from the top
of her spectacles at all of us in the throes of awkward adolescence, she commanded both fear and respect. Mrs. Lovejoy was
passionate about not just what she taught but also about those
whom she taught.

In eighth grade Mrs. Lovejoy read a story I'd written for an
assignment to the whole class. She didn't read anyone else's.
Just mine. The story was about an old lady who fed the birds in the
park every day. Kids made fun of her, but the main character of
the story, a girl about my age, didn't poke fun at the old bird lady.

Instead the girl just watched and learned from her. Then the old lady in the story died, and the girl took her place in the park, feeding the birds. That's how the story ended. When Mrs. Lovejoy read the story to our class, she cried. My classmates thought my story was stupid, because they had already heard of stories of old people feeding birds in the park, they said. They didn't see what was so different about mine and they didn't understand what Mrs. Lovejoy had gotten all choked up about. But I knew, and Mrs. Lovejoy knew. Much as it hurt that my classmates didn't appreciate my story, that's all that really mattered.

That same year, Mrs. Lovejoy introduced me to Charles Dickens' *Great Expectations*. It wasn't the real *Great Expectations*, but an abridged, illustrated edition for younger readers. Some people think that to abridge a classic work of literature is an act of sacrilege, but my junior high experience of reading an abridged *Great Expectations* might be likened to a child's first communion: a step taken in immature faith toward a fuller, richer experience to come. Besides, now that I've followed in Mrs. Lovejoy's footsteps and become an English teacher myself, I've found among some of my college students that they have come to hate some of the classic works they read in middle and high school simply because they weren't ready to appreciate the subtleties and complexities of such works. This was exactly my own experience in reading *Pride and Prejudice* the first time. Since the most dramatic thing that ever happens in an Austen novel is that "a man changes his manners and a woman changes her mind," as it's put on the back cover of the Penguin Classics edition, one must have both a mind and manners in order to appreciate such a plot. Evidently, in the ninth grade when I first read it, I was lacking in both, and I rolled my eyes a lot in class while Miss Green waxed enthusiastically about how witty Elizabeth Bennet was. Thankfully, my lack then was supplied over time, and I have overcome my first impression of *Pride and Prejudice*.

An abridged version is merely the gateway drug to the real thing. Even in its shortened form, *Great Expectations* presented itself as quite a daunting tome for a middle-school student. But the story grabbed my attention from the very beginning, all the way to the end. Even more than the book's illustrations, the mental pictures I formed of the scenes, conjured like magic from the words on the pages, remain with me today. The most vivid of these images is of a withered and yellowed Miss Havisham looming over a petrified wedding cake, both she and it entombed in a decaying mansion since the very hour—8:40, to be exact—at which her betrothed abandoned her many years before, on what was supposed to have been her wedding day. It was remarkable how much Miss Havisham resembled Mrs. Lovejoy. Mrs. Lovejoy hadn't been jilted, but she had been widowed many years before, which was almost as tantalizing. I could never forget Dickens' description of that rotten, virginal wedding cake, crawling with speckled spiders or the maze of tangled weeds and overgrown brush that encased the crumbling sepulchre of a mansion called, ironically, Satis House—*enough,* in Latin. Or young Pip shivering alone among the gravestones of his deceased father, mother, and siblings in a desolate graveyard on the marshes. Or Pip's scuffle with the ghostly Pale Young Gentleman on the grounds of Satis House. These images are as vivid in my mind as the memories of real people and real events in my life. This is part of the magic of story.

The next time I read *Great Expectations* was in high school. This was the unabridged version, and our teacher even required us to purchase our own paperback copies—just like college students. I still have that copy of the book among the many other editions I now own. According to the price stamped on the cover, it cost $2.50. Many years later in graduate school, I used that very same volume. It's in pretty rough shape now and smells more like a musty attic than a book. The pages have surpassed the stage of mere yellowing and have turned a brownish tobacco color, and chunks of them have separated from the binding. Its covers are encased in clear contact paper, which has held remarkably well, in an attempt I made at some point to lengthen its life. For a while I held it together by wrapping it with a rubber band, but the band caused the pages to tear. I retired it to the shelf where it will comfortably live out the rest of its life next to other paperbacks like George Eliot's *Middlemarch* and my first copy of *Jane Eyre.*

I still like to look at this battered old book now and then, for the pages contain more than the story itself. In sparse places it has notes made in my large, round teenage-girl handwriting (making me grateful that I never went through a stage of dotting my "i"s with circles or, more dreadfully, hearts). The print is girlish enough and unhurried, consisting largely of character names and major plot events: "Miss Havisham's Story," for example, and "Camilla." It's easy to tell which notes I made later on in graduate school, not only by the significantly narrowed and less legible handwriting, but also by the words themselves, which consist of terms and phrases like "cinematic," "fragility of authority," "ritualized violence," and "central human gesture." There are at least four different colors of ink in the book, a sign of the book's constancy in my life.

It's always been hard for me to pick out my "favorite" book in the broadest sense of the term. I can easily identify "the book that most influenced my life" (that's for a later chapter) or "my favorite book to teach" or "my favorite play by an American playwright" or "the most important novel of the eighteenth century," and so on. But my all time, no-qualifiers-limiters-or-descriptors favorite? I've never really been able to narrow that down to fewer than three. But I guess if someone were to kidnap one of my dogs and demand as ransom that I choose one favorite book, my choice would have to be *Great Expectations.* I have lost track of how many times I have read it, but I still find myself laughing, tearing up, and making delightful new discoveries with each fresh reading.

What I love most about *Great Expectations* is its sheer magic. Dickens has a way of presenting both plot and characters that are enchanting enough to set the imagination aflame but at the same time realistic enough to reflect life as it really is, or might really be, at least. In other words, I can take pure pleasure in the story, but at the same time I know I need to pay attention as I read, for within are important truths about human nature and the human condition. For the real magic of this story is the way in which it shows the magic that can be found, not only in the pages of the book but all around me in everyday life and everyday love.

This magical quality is seen first and most obviously in the characters of the novel. They are, paradoxically, realistic caricatures. Dickens' characters are fanciful and at the same time just like someone you probably know or might see on the streets of any town. G. K. Chesterton answered the charge of some critics that the idiosyncrasies of Dickens' characters are too exaggerated by predicting, "It will be proved that he is hardly even a caricaturist; that he is something very like a realist. Those comic monstrosities which the critics found incredible will be found to be the immense majority of the citizens of this country." I think Chesterton was right. What child has not had even an indirect encounter with a reclusive Miss Havisham-like spinster surrounded in some real or imagined mystery? Who doesn't have an uncle or some other torturous relative such as Pumblechook who is eager to blame the young for every conceivable (and even inconceivable) social ill? And who hasn't marveled at the way the neglectful parenting of certain fecund women like Mrs. Pocket results in their swarm of children "tumbling up," quite miraculously without death or serious injury? And I hope everyone has been blessed to know a kind and generous craftsman in the pattern of Joe, a man who takes pride in his work, but not in himself, a man simple but wise, forbearing and forgiving...but I am getting ahead of myself.

One of the most interesting characters in *Great Expectations* is actually a minor one, Mr. Wemmick, who serves as clerk to Mr. Jaggers, lawyer and legal guardian of Pip once Pip comes into his "great expectations" at the hands of an anonymous benefactor. When Pip first encounters Wemmick in his official capacity as clerk, Pip remarks, "I found him to be a dry man, rather short in stature, with a square wooden face, whose expression seems to have been imperfectly chipped out with a dull-edged chisel." Later Pip says of Wemmick, "His mouth was such a post office of a mouth that he had a mechanical appearance of smiling." This "mechanical," "post office" mouth is emblematic of Wemmick, the modern professional man (a phenomenon of Dickens' Victorian England), carrying out his job with all the heart of an automaton.

Pip comes to learn that there is more to Wemmick than his professional persona, upon being invited to visit Wemmick at home, the only place where he will discuss matters of a personal rather than business nature. There, Pip discovers a completely different side of the law clerk. In a miniature gothic castle—cut off from the outside world by a drawbridge over a four-foot wide ditch—Wemmick makes for himself and his Aged Parent a most warm and hospitable, if peculiar, home. Here the officious clerk melts into doting son, eager suitor of the virtuous Miss Skiffins, and a regular jack-of-all-trades. Here at home, Wemmick's post office mouth loosens and opens, allowing Wemmick to provide, happily, his personal sentiments and advice. But later, as Pip accompanies Wemmick from his Walworth home back to the law office, Pip notices, "By degrees, Wemmick got dryer and harder as we went along, and his mouth tightened into a post office again." On a later occasion, Pip attempts to solicit a personal opinion from Wemmick in the professional setting, thus ignoring the boundaries Wemmick has drawn as tightly as the lips of his post office mouth between his public and private lives. Wemmick chastises Pip, saying, "Walworth is one place, and this office is another. . .They must not be confounded together. My Walworth sentiments must be taken at Walworth; none but my official sentiments can be taken in this office."

Surely Wemmick is one of the most comical—even exaggerated—characters in the novel (and perhaps in all of Dickens). Yet, at the same time, he is one of the most realistic of characters in that he accurately reflects the conflicted state of modern man. Wemmick might be said to be the quintessential modern man, and, with closer examination of a character that on the surface seems utterly ridiculous, we realize that perhaps he is not so ridiculous after all. Modern life is characterized by nothing if not an efficient and practical compartmentalization of its distinct spheres: public and private, sacred and secular, scientific and religious, physical and spiritual. Dickens's caricature of such compartmentalization in the character of Wemmick is humorous to be sure, but it still reflects the truth, even if that reflection is cast by a funhouse mirror. The compartmentalization of our own lives may not be as concretely marked as Wemmick's post office mouth that tightens and loosens as he goes from one sphere to the next, but there may be other, subtler, more serious markers. Perhaps it is not the character of Wemmick that is absurd but rather the compartmentalization of life in the modern age.

Absurd or not, this kind of compartmentalization is hard to escape. It's everywhere around us and sometimes in us. It wasn't until I'd read *Great Expectations* many times that I recognized in real life what Dickens shows us in the character of Wemmick. On the surface, yes, he depicts a man who has deeply divided his work life and his home life. That's not entirely a bad thing, but it is a distinct characteristic of the modern age. In contrast, in the pre-modern agrarian age the workplace and the home hearth were knit together more closely. It seems the postmodern technological age allows us to do the same, if we wish. Perhaps we should.

There is also a visceral sort of compartmentalization, one that Dickens shows us more subtly through the character of Wemmick. This one not only divides our public self from our private self but also divides us into various selves, often in ways we don't even recognize. I think, for example, of how by high school I had become one person when I was partying with my friends and another when I was going to church with my parents. That's natural of teenage rebellion—it's not like I could light up a joint in church so as to live a de-compartmentalized life. But there are more insidious manifestations to this compartmentalized life. When my youth group leader told all of the kids in youth group that he had burned all of his rock albums, and I happened to listen to rock music, I saw two choices before me: either to burn all my albums, too, or to keep listening but not talk about it in church on Sunday or with any of my Sunday friends. I chose the latter, not seeing a third option of voicing disagreement or engaging in further discussion. My choice made it more difficult to share my Sunday life with my non-Sunday friends and therefore only fortified the partitions that chopped my life into bits.

A subtle divide easily becomes a rigid compartmentalization, a post office mouth that communicates different selves in different spheres. A divided self is an imprisoned self; little respite is offered by a Walworth-style bridge between two worlds or two selves. This is why some years later when I was a teacher in a private high school, I gave an exercise to my students in which I typed up lines from a variety of popular songs, handed them out, and asked the students to analyze the beliefs and worldviews expressed, without any titles or artists to help them. I wanted my students to see that a holistic approach to life examines all things critically, apart from whatever pre-existing compartments or labels they come with. Applying the principles underlying one's beliefs to all things—which is neither to embrace nor reject something in and of itself—is a more holistic approach to all of life.

This is the essence of truth Wemmick shows, but besides all that he is simply a delightful and quirky character whom I never tire of meeting in the pages of the book.

In terms of the story itself, there is so much more than even this unforgettable character. Without giving too much away to anyone who has yet to read it, suffice it to say that the ending of *Great Expectations* is fairly realistic, another aspect of the story I appreciate. By realistic I mean it's neither overly cheery nor tragically maudlin. It's, well, a lot like real life: some bad things happen, some good things happen, and Pip at last learns to make the best of it all.

Perhaps I should mention that there are actually two endings: Dickens' original ending and the one his publisher wanted. Most editions now include both. What I am saying here applies to both versions despite their significant differences.

Sure, many of the events of the book turn on coincidence and improbability—which is consistent with Dickens's own faith, which supports the idea of a providential God who intervenes in human affairs—but the outcome of all these events is fairly reflective of life in this world. The events show that we can really screw up (that's Pip's part), receive forgiveness (like that offered him by Joe) and experience regeneration (as seen in little Pip Jr.), but some of the natural consequences of sin cannot be entirely repaired in this human realm. Despite what some critics might say about the improbabilities of the plot, its pattern is the very pattern of human existence: fall, redemption, and the working out of our salvation in this blighted world until our complete restoration in the next one.

Novels—my favorite genre of literature for this very reason—
are, in fact, about this very process of finding ourselves once we
have fallen away from God. As C. S. Lewis is credited with saying,
"We read to know we are not alone." The greatest form of loneliness is separation from God. The Hungarian critic Georg Lukacs
says that the novel is the literary genre for the soul in search of its
home. Lukacs describes the human condition before the soul's
lapse from God this way:

> When the soul does not yet know any abyss
> within itself which may tempt it to fall or en-
> courage it to discover pathless heights, when the
> divinity that rules the world and distributes the
> unknown and unjust gifts of destiny is not yet un-
> derstood by man, but is familiar and close to him
> as a father is to his small child, then every action
> is only a well-fitting garment for the world. Being
> and destiny, adventure and accomplishment, life
> and essence are then identical concepts.

According to Lukacs, in both its form and its content, novels express the soul's attempt to transcend this "abyss." The search for
identity and meaning is one way we attempt to cross this chasm,
to find our way home. "There's no place like home" to be utterly
free—home free.

One of the most profound means by which we seek our way
back home is through the search for meaning in our lives and
in the world around us. This human impulse to find oneself in
relation to the surrounding world is depicted quite literally in
Great Expectations in a comical—but deeply meaningful—scene in
which young Pip learns that his brother-in-law/surrogate father,
the blacksmith Joe, cannot read. One evening at the fireside, Pip,
who is just learning to read and write himself, manages to scrib-
ble out a short, phonetically spelled missive on his little slate.
He proudly hands it to Joe to read. "Why here's a J and a O,
Pip and a J-O, Joe," exults the blacksmith. Pip realizes now for the
first time that Joe is illiterate (which explains to Pip why it is that

Joe is no less inconvenienced while holding the Prayer-book in church upside down as right side up). But what Pip fails to grasp is the fact that just because Joe is illiterate does not mean that he cannot read in a metaphysical sense. Indeed Joe is a greater reader of people and life than Pip ever is able to become. As the scene continues, Joe protests to Pip that he can in fact read:

> "Give me . . . a good book, or a good newspaper, and sit me down afore a good fire, and I ask no better. Lord!" he continued, after rubbing his knees a little "when you do come to a J and a O, and says you, 'Here, at last, is a J-O, Joe' how interesting reading is!"

We laugh at Joe's simplicity and his egocentrism—reading a text merely to spot the letters of his own name without understanding the remainder—but then isn't that what we all do when we read? Don't we, in fact, like Joe, read in order to find ourselves? Sure, we learn about other people, other places, other ideas in the process, but ultimately isn't it, as Lukacs says, all in the attempt to bring our souls home? The more we read, the better readers we become: we've heard that all our lives. There's another layer of meaning to that truism. Not only do we become more literate when we read, but we also become better interpreters—or readers—of human life and human nature.

That's a fact I never fully comprehended until one of my closest friends, whose profession and lifestyle are of a decidedly unliterary nature, pointed it out to me. "Because you read so much," she told me one day, "you're a better interpreter of life."

The more I thought about it, the more I realized that reading—that is, really reading, interpreting—literature is practice for reading and interpreting life. The more one practices, the better one gets. This is why excellent novels such as *Great Expectations* are not only books to be read, but they are also books about reading—just as Joe searches for the letters of his name and Pip reads the tombstones of his deceased mother, father, and brothers in the opening scene. This kind of reading is the act of interpreting our individual lives within the context of the larger world. It is the search for meaning.

It's a kind of alchemy, really, the way dark lines on white paper—or before paper, engraved in stone, and after paper, crystallized on a screen—cause images and ideas to appear like magic in our minds.

The human impulse to create and find meaning is a gift of grace. Grace is the opposite of "expectations" because it is so, well, unexpected. And, interestingly enough, grace is at the center of *Great Expectations.*

In contrast to the expectations Pip comes into as a payback for the actions he unwittingly performed for his unknown benefactor, grace comes entirely unexpected and undeserved. It comes embodied in the form of Joe, Pip's brother-in-law and surrogate parent. Now, I'm not the kind of reader who goes hunting for Christ-figures in every book, but I'd have to be pretty thick not to see, after so many readings, some unexpected parallels to Christ in unlikely Joe. First, Joe is a blacksmith, a literary type often linked with a Creator who forged the world and humankind out of a fiery but benevolent power that fuels the universe. Furthermore, Joe alone in the story offers Pip unconditional and unwavering love. The light from Joe's forge is for Pip always a warm beckoning toward home even before Pip recognizes it as such. In addition, Joe's love language (to invoke the Christian cliché), like God's, is food.

Just as God's early words to his human creation as recorded in Genesis were "Eat freely," an act reinforced later in the New Testament with the command to remember the sacrifice of Christ with the food and drink of the communion table, so Joe seeks, in an environment boasting no luxuries or niceties, to bless Pip with something as simple and good as food.

Pip describes how Joe "always aided and comforted me when he could, in some way of his own, and he always did so at dinnertime by giving me gravy, if there were any." And the more Joe senses that Pip is in need of love or comfort, the more he spoons gravy onto Pip's plate. Joe is also the only thing that Pip has ever truly believed in, even if Pip does eventually fall away for a while.

For a time anyway, Joe is home to Pip's lonely soul. Pip even describes the place of Joe in his life in the form of a sort of creed:

> Home had never been a very pleasant place to me, because of my sister's temper. But Joe had sanctified it, and I believed in it. I had believed in the best parlour as a most elegant saloon; I had believed in the front door as a mysterious portal of the Temple of State whose opening was attended with a sacrifice of roust fowls; I had believed in the kitchen as a chaste though not magnificent apartment; I had believed in the forge as the glowing road to manhood and independence.

Remarkably, as ancient as she had seemed to my classmates and me more than two decades before, Mrs. Lovejoy was still around, although long retired, when I returned to Maine some summers ago and called upon her at home one Sunday after church. The smell of chicken and rice wafted in from Mrs. Lovejoy's kitchen as she and I sat in the living room. If she was distracted by her dinner cooking, she never let it show. I didn't stay long. I wanted to thank her for her tremendous influence in my life and give her a copy of my first book, a scholarly work based on my doctoral dissertation, the kind of book no one really reads. She received it with tears that beckoned mine, and it occurred to me that she had been, in her way, a home to my soul. I'm glad I didn't put that visit off, for Mrs. Lovejoy died just a few months later.

A short time after Pip's brief homily, when he confesses to Joe a lie he had told, Joe's response is exactly what I have always imagined God's to be at our sin: disbelief followed by disappointment, then firm but gentle chastisement. And it's Joe's disbelief at Pip's sin that always grips my heart. Just as Joe genuinely expects more of Pip, so God has "great expectations" for his children, in terms of both what he wants from us and, more importantly, what he wants for us.

Joe reflects Christ on a level deeper than mere characterization and actions. Even more profoundly, the very rhythm of Joe's presence in Pip's life echoes the rhythm of my own recognition of God's presence in my life. As a child, Pip took Joe's constant, loving presence for granted, much as I, growing up in the church, took God's constant, loving presence for granted. This is what helped me to compartmentalize my life with such ease, to be a good church kid on Sunday and something else the rest of the week. Pip takes Joe's love for granted, too. Upon bestowal of his "expectations," Pip embarks on a journey of becoming a gentleman and, in the process, grows ashamed of Joe and eventually abandons him, not just physically but, more poignantly, emotionally.

Yet, later, when Pip becomes sick and desperately in need, it is Joe who rescues him. While Pip spends weeks in bed, in and out of a delirious fever, he recalls the faces of the friends who have surrounded him during his illness:

> ...there was a constant tendency in all these people, sooner or later, to settle down into the likeness of Joe.

> After I had turned the worse point of my illness, I began to notice that while all its other features changed, this one consistent feature did not change. Whoever came about me, still settled down into Joe. I opened my eyes in the day, and, sitting on the window-seat, smoking his pipe in the shaded open window, still I saw Joe. I asked for a cooling drink, and the face that looked so hopefully and tenderly upon me was the face of Joe.

> At last, one day, I took courage, and said, "Is it Joe?"

> And the dear old home-voice answered, "Which it air, old chap."

> "Oh, Joe, you break my heart! Look angry at me, Joe. Strike me, Joe. Tell me of my ingratitude.

> Don't be so good to me!" For Joe had actually laid
> his head down on the pillow at my side, and put
> his arm round my neck, in his joy that I knew him.

Surely, this is a picture God, who is said to be longsuffering, stretching out his hand for us to grasp the very moment we will. This passage touches me more deeply each time I read it.

I admit that my relationship with God has been more intellectual than emotional. I used to think this lack of emotional fervor was a mark of sin or, at the very least, some great flaw in my spiritual life. I thought that it must be a great lack in my faith that I am more emotionally moved in reading literary works like *Great Expectations* than in reading dramatic passages in the bible or in hearing a moving testimony from the pulpit. But I've come to realize that my emotional responses to moving works of literature, like the passage above, are the only way I can bear to respond emotionally to God and his love: indirectly.

It's like when Moses asked God to see his glory, and God answered, "You cannot see my face, for man shall not see me and live." So God took Moses to the cleft of a rock and covered him with his hand while his glory passed by. As R. C. Sproul notes about this passage, "The Lord's goodness withheld what Moses could not bear and revealed all that he could." To respond emotionally to God directly is more than I can bear. So God in his goodness has bestowed the gift of literature. Literature is like the cleft of a rock that God has taken me to, a place from which I can experience as much of the glory of God as I can endure. Great literature allows me, like Moses, to see the back of God.

Not everyone loves English or reading literature or their eighth-grade English teacher or their college professors. Not everyone loves *Great Expectations*. My cousin will not let me forget the summer she "wasted" trying to get through *Great Expectations* because I had so strongly recommended it. She is a voracious reader of popular fiction—I count as one the best accomplishments of my youth that I introduced her to the joys of reading one summer when we were about 10, a couple of summers before she and her older sister introduced me to the joys of sneaking puffs of cigarettes out in our Grampa's woods—and, seeking to give her reading a more literary turn, she asked me for suggestions. I don't think she'll ever do so again. But I suspect that the pleasure she takes in reminding me of her lost summer just might make up for the lack of pleasure she found in actually reading the book. Other friends, too, have picked up the book at my bidding, only to put it quietly down again after torturously slow starts.

Not everyone appreciates the magic of *Great Expectations*, but that's the thing about magic: it doesn't work on everyone. In order for magic to work, first you have to believe. This passage in *Great Expectations* about Joe's Christ-like love is one I always read aloud when I teach this novel, usually during the last class we will spend on the book. One semester, the class I taught was unusually large. The course had become popular in the department, and I was always willing to sign high-achieving students into the class no matter how overfilled it had become. Because the class was not only large but also populated with an abundance of well-read, confident, and loquacious students (several of whom were on the university's champion debate team), our classes were always lively— sometimes downright boisterous. One student practically turned Pip-hostility into a sport. Later, after he had graduated and become a mission worker in Guatemala, he emailed me to tell me that he had just read Dickens' *A Tale of Two Cities*—and loved it. That was a partial victory: at least Dickens, if not *Great Expectations,* was redeemed.

But on the day we were covering this part of the book, when I got to this passage and began to read, the class immediately turned hushed and rapt. I hadn't prepped them for the significance of this part of the story to the work as a whole, but they must have sensed it. I looked up briefly from my reading. As I stood reading, my students were all gazing steadily and seriously at me. Even the chronic note passers. Then as I looked down to continue reading, something unexpected happened, something that had never happened while I was teaching: I felt my eyes begin to water, and I heard the slightest waver in my voice. I had worked hard thus far in my still-young academic career to establish and maintain a reputation for toughness, the sort that will attract the best students, repel the others, and make those that do take the plunge excel beyond their (and hopefully my) expectations. Crying in class is not the sort of thing that aids this endeavor. Nor is it my style. So I focused hard, concentrated on my vocal delivery rather than on the meaning of the words, and willed my eyes to draw the moisture back in as I continued to read. When I finished and looked up from the page at the preternaturally quiet students, I was stunned to see several students sitting in their seats look up at me with tears streaming down their faces.

Tears returned to my eyes as I mentally journeyed back, to my eighth-grade classroom at Monmouth Academy. Mrs. Lovejoy stood at the front of the very room where I read *Great Expectations* for the first time. She was reading a short story, one I had written, about an old lady who fed birds, and Mrs. Lovejoy was crying. I knew that day in front of my own students part of her was with me, weeping as a young girl took an old woman's place scattering food for the gathered.

5

Beholding is Becoming: *Jane Eyre*

I took a deep breath and listened to the old bray
of my heart. I am. I am. I am.

—Sylvia Plath

Lunchtime at Monmouth Academy accommodated grades seven
through twelve for public school students in my rural Maine
hometown. The pillared brick building reflected the dignity of the
school's name and sat on an expanse of green lawn, guarded by
leafy trees. Built in 1803, the school had no cafeteria. Students
wanting what was called "hot lunch" had to ride the bus a short
way down the road to the elementary school. However, the only
kids who did that were those whose meals were subsidized by the
federal school lunch program. The rest of us wouldn't be caught
dead taking the bus to the cafeteria. We brought our own lunches
or ordered delivery from the local pizzeria, a nice benefit of attending a school too small for a cafeteria.

I carried my usual paper bag, which toted a sandwich, chips,
and a container of yogurt, into a classroom where several girls sat
at desks arranged in a circle, and took a deep breath. This was
going to be one of the most humbling moments in my fourteen
years of life.

*

Eighth is the cruelest grade. Cruel in so many ways, but nearly all
ways boiling down to the fact that this is the age of the halfling.
The age of *becoming,* with little notion of what it is one is supposed
to become. Over the course of the first part of this, my eighth

grade year, it had become clear—slowly, painfully, awkwardly—that I no longer fit in with the popular girls I'd been hanging around with since sixth grade when all of the girls in my class had formed cliques. Our school was so small that there were only two classes for each grade. The girls in my grade divided into three groups: the cool girls, the smart girls, and the nobodies who were everybody else.

Somehow, somewhere, someone had made a mistake, and I had ended up with the cool girls.

I think it started in sixth grade on the playground during recess when I helped some of the others protect the leader of the pack (the only one among us who'd reached a certain fullness of bodily development) from the boys who chased her on the playground, taunting her with the nickname "Peach Fuzz" and trying to pin her down and kiss her. Someone had to explain to me the nickname, which I deemed too stupid to be true, until a couple of years later when I had a better understanding of the situation. Still, I couldn't quite figure out, based on this odd behavior, if the boys liked Peach Fuzz or disliked her.

Anyway, we cool girls called ourselves, simply, The Group, not realizing how much this made us sound like something from a segment of an After School Special that got left on the cutting room floor. In The Group, you were either in or you were out. Period. Sometimes people who were in got kicked out through a culling process that made cockfights look civilized. At any rate, I was in but had yet to learn that group membership and true friendship are not the same thing.

This was a lesson *Jane Eyre,* the title character of Charlotte Brontë's nineteenth century novel, didn't have to learn. Surrounded in early life by people she'd never mistake for friends, it was a long time before Jane had anyone she could even consider a friend. By the time I met Jane for the first time in my sophomore English class, I had learned a bit more about friendship. And because of Jane, I was going to learn a lot more about myself.

For the purposes of sheer pedantry, one could hardly do better than *Jane Eyre* to deliver a scattershot of literary movements and terms. The novel displays elements of romanticism, gothicism, realism, allegory, satire, and—most fittingly for the adolescent reader—the *bildungsroman,* or "coming of age" novel.

While most of my literary-minded peers of that time were charmed by the higher Romanticism of Charlotte's sister Emily in *Wuthering Heights,* I much preferred the greater realism of *Jane Eyre.* That's not to say that Eyre's Romantic elements—the detainment of a young girl in the frightening bedroom of a long dead inhabitant; an omen-laden lightning strike down the middle of a great tree; the inexplicable, audible voice of a lover calling from miles away; and the mysterious mad woman in the attic—didn't enchant me. I could certainly be as dreamy as the next teenage girl. *Jane Eyre* has a little bit of everything in it, enough to appeal to bookish girls of nearly all tastes since its publication a century and a half ago.

Such a bookish friend of mine recalls that at about the age of twelve, she turned her general dissatisfaction with life typical of most twelve-year-olds into a fascination with Jane. Like Jane, she began sitting in corners and observing people. She took up drawing and "developed an interest in gruff, hairy men."

"I am reasonably certain," my friend added, "I was unbearable then." Though she never outgrew her love of *Jane Eyre,* she did, I'm happy to say, eventually move out of the corners and into the teaching profession and married a gentle, clean-cut man much closer to her own age.

Despite these romantic and escapist elements, the center of *Jane Eyre,* the heroine of that name, is one of the most realistic characters I had yet encountered in the considerable number of novels I had read up to that time. For, unlike most literary heroines, Jane Eyre is not striking, beautiful, or even pretty. In fact, Jane Eyre is quite remarkable in being quite plain. The fact is that Charlotte Brontë specifically set out to create just such a character, an act no less than revolutionary for a novel-writer of the time. Her friend, biographer, and fellow novelist Elizabeth Gaskell, reports Brontë proclaiming of Jane, "I will show you a heroine as plain and small as myself, who shall be as interesting as any of yours." But even beyond mere physical appearance Jane is a realistic, not an idealistic, figure.

Centuries of English and European literary tradition had offered up female characters who were angels or whores, pure or fallen, damsels or crones. In stark relief, Jane Eyre is one of the first female characters to fall uncomfortably—realistically—in the middle position between utter perfection and hopeless ruin, the place where all mere mortals are to be found. She is neither sweet nor complaisant, but strong-willed and determined. Nor is she wretched and fallen, but a faithful and sincere Christian. "I am not an angel," Jane asserts, "and I will not be one till I die: I will be myself."

Sometime between seventh and eighth grades a deep dark secret about me began to leak out. The secret was that, despite being a member of The Group, I really wasn't very cool. For one thing, I liked school. Not just riding the bus, taking recess, passing notes, and giggling, but school. I was so excited about my sixth grade science project that on the same day it was assigned I went home, piled up the books on my father's big roll top desk, and got to work. Even though we had the entire grading period to work on it, I finished it in a week or two. I cared what my teachers thought about me. Even worse, I cared about what they thought more than I cared what my friends thought. Such misplaced priorities do not make for a wildly successful middle school social life. Plus, I played by myself a lot and liked it, too, though I didn't consider spending time with my horses, my cats, or my rabbits as really being by myself. And, unlike most of my classmates, I went to church every Sunday.

When I did try to fit in better, I ended up off by a step. One year when vests were in, I had my mother make me a tan corduroy one, only to be chastised by Peach Fuzz, who was originally from New York City where, she told us, she'd been friends with Brooke Shields. Apparently, the blouse I wore with the vest was too bright a shade of yellow. When I tried out for the cheerleading squad along with the rest of The Group upon entering seventh grade, everyone made the squad but me. I didn't even make alternate. Yet, somehow I had managed to keep up the coolness charade throughout the seventh grade.

Nevertheless, the summer between seventh and eighth grades, something happened, and I got left behind. Whatever it was that each of us was becoming, it seemed that, despite my fervent desire otherwise, I was becoming something other than them. When we went back to school that fall of eighth grade, the leaders of The Group returned in possession of boyfriends from other schools, older boys. The stories the girls told about the things they had done that summer with those boyfriends surprised me a little, though I tried not to let it show. I made a valiant effort to be cool, on the surface anyway, but it was hard sometimes to hide my decidedly uncool views.

Sitting in the lounge where we always had lunch, some joker tuned the radio to a country station instead of the usual classic rock. We didn't know anyone who actually listened to country music.

No one listened to country music.

A Willie Nelson song played over the loudspeakers. The lounge was a one-room metal building equipped with pool tables, chairs and couches, a bar where the students could buy drinks and snacks, and a loudspeaker playing the coolest rock station in central Maine. It was the coolest place to eat lunch, and we were the only kids in junior high who dared to join the high schoolers there. Of course, we didn't get to play pool, but we could watch while sitting atop the backs of overstuffed chairs with our feet resting on the seats and passing around a bag of Humpty Dumpty potato chips. One of the girls in The Group began to laugh. She said the song reminded her of something funny her stepfather had said the night before to his friends over beers.

One of the stepfather's friends had asked all of them what they would wish for if they could have anything in the world. The stepfather answered, "A whole field of Dolly Partons!"

Everyone in The Group seemed to think that was really funny. I instantly pictured row after row of enormous bare breasts pointing up in the air like conical cornstalks. "That's a stupid thing to wish for," I said, without really stopping to think if it was stupid of me to say so.

Everyone grew quiet and stared at me.

"I mean, if you could wish for anything in the world, why wouldn't you wish for something important?" This is the kind of sauciness that had gotten me kicked out of math class for a day and junior high chorus for good.

"It was just a joke!" Stepdaughter said, disdainfully, rolling her eyes, while the others squinted at me and continued to insert potato chips between their pursed lips and chomp noisily.

Being too serious is another thing I've always had trouble with.

That was the trouble. The things I liked, they thought were stupid. The things they thought were funny and cool, I thought were stupid. Consequently, I spent a lot of time thinking about how stupid a lot of things were which is not a good way to make or keep friends. To this day, despite my great efforts to prevent it, I occasionally will have a student complain that I make him or her "feel stupid." It's a flaw I had then and have now although the consequences are different now—most of the time. And I care more now to correct it than I did then.

Before long, I was kicked out of The Group.

The funny thing was that nearly everyone else had been kicked out of The Group before this at one point or another, even Stepdaughter and she was one of the leaders. What usually happened with a Kick Out was that the outcast would just kind of hang around on the outskirts, striking some sort of balance between looking adequately repentant—but still cool—until enough time and punishment had passed as penance for whatever crime had been committed, or until someone else was more deserving of disgrace, and the offending member was unceremoniously permitted re-entrance.

Despite the fact that I'd seen this cycle repeated numerous times, when it was my turn for excommunication, I didn't come crawling back. It wasn't a conscious decision, though. Hurt as I was, I was not bitter or vengeful. I might not be cool, but I had self-respect. I honestly didn't want to be where I wasn't wanted. So when the day came when these girls turned on me, I didn't play the game. I took my stand. And in the eighth grade such a stand can take no more revolutionary, no more dramatic or resistant, a form than to eat lunch somewhere else.

*

This was how I found myself at lunchtime in another classroom, in another building, far away from The Group with whom I'd been friends for one quarter of my school years. The fact that our school didn't have a cafeteria where everyone would be, turned out to be a small mercy. Students simply congregated in the school lounge or in empty classrooms, one clique per room. At least I could take my stand without being under the scrutinizing eyes of the rest of the school or, more unthinkably, The Group.

Lunch bag in hand, I took a deep breath and asked the Smart Girls if I could eat with them.

They said yes.

It wasn't a completely seamless merger. The Smart Girls had even less fashion sense than I did. Only one of them wore make-up, and she wore it so ineptly that she looked like a clown. But who was I to judge, I of the too-bright-yellow shirt? The Smart Girls apparently didn't go to any parties, at least not ones with boys, but they were kind to me. And interesting, too.

Like me, they relished learning and studying, and they cared about their grades. School was, for the time being at least, still more important than clothes or boys. Soon the Smart Girls were my friends. One of them, like me, went on to become a professor. Another, Rachael, became my best friend, and our friendship continues to this day.

Hanging around with these bookish girls surely set me on a different course, a path easier to recognize looking back now than it was in its midst. By high school, I became more focused on academics than I'd ever been. Our tenth grade English teacher, Miss Green, was young, not jaded, and eager to teach us great literature. She wore corduroy jumpers, sensible shoes, and an earnest face. She harbored great expectations for her students and assigned many classic works to us that year.

But *Jane Eyre* is the one I remember most.

Like Jane, I had a very strong sense of self from a young age. Unlike Jane, however, my strong sense of self was nourished by my parents. Even so, I did not feel—because I was not—self-possessed; I had a sense of who I was, but I wasn't yet comfortable in my own skin. Outside the protective buffer of parental love and encouragement, I, like Jane, had a sense of not really belonging. I was sufficiently like the rest of the kids to have friends enough and social opportunities enough, but whether I was with the cool girls in The Group or, later, the Smart Girls, I still didn't feel like I exactly fit in. It was quite a challenge for a girl plain and small like me to be interesting to and among others who seemed—agonizingly—not so plain, not so uninteresting, not so ill-fitted to everyone else around me.

Deep down I knew I was just as interesting as they, but I was also painfully aware that all that showed on the outside was a bespectacled, befreckled, baby-fatted girl with lumpy hair, one too ill-coordinated to make either the cheerleading squad or the basketball team, who clunked heavily up the bleachers rather than springing gracefully like the other girls. One who sat on those bleachers through every basketball game reading books while everyone else was cheering and clapping. One who could hang with the popular girls but never feel at home with them. One who could never say no to Mr. Taylor, my sixth grade English and History teacher, who always asked me to work with Caroline, the slow girl in our class, simply because I was one of the few classmates who was kind to her. One who wished to not to care so much what the cool kids or the smart kids thought—but did.

I did not see then that adolescence is to some extent isolating for everyone, even the shiny-haired, smooth-skinned girls and the athletic, poised, unclumsy girls, and the girls the boys flocked around, and the girls who got the highest grades all the time—girls not like me. Just as Leo Tolstoy famously observed in *Anna Karenina,* that "happy families are all alike; every unhappy family is unhappy in its own way," the unhappiness of adolescence is unique to each one.

Even so, Jane Eyre seemed in so many ways to be someone like me. In reading and studying the book many more times later in life, I came to realize that this was because she really was. And, truth be told, a lot like the other girls, too, because *Jane Eyre* is really about every adolescent. For adolescence, more than any other age, is a time of *becoming,* when we all must navigate through endless possibilities of being and overcome countless temptations to become any person but one that reflects both the givenness of our being and the possibilities of our becoming.

This search for the self is characteristic of the modern condition, and it is no coincidence that one of the first modern individuals in literature was a woman. Throughout history women have embodied, more dramatically and sooner than men, changing cultural ideas and conditions. There was no more dramatic cultural change during the time in which *Jane Eyre* was written than that which brought about the rise of the individual. Precisely because of an inferior place in society throughout all of human history to this point, no figure better depicted the rise of the modern individual than the woman. So while in the traditional Romances such as those of the Arthurian legends it is the noblemen, the knights in shining armor, who embark on a quest, in *Jane Eyre* it is a poor friendless woman who is on the greatest quest of all: the quest for the self.

This is what makes the novel a *bildungsroman,* a story of education, struggle, loss, and of finding one's place in the world. Jane's journey is a journey to authentic selfhood. It is the same journey that every modern young person must undergo. I did not know that the truest sense of belonging comes from feeling like you belong to yourself because of who you were created to be. I was what one Old Testament passage says of the wandering Israelites: an alien and a pilgrim.

In the ancient and medieval worlds, people gained their identities not from their individuality but from their communities: the families they were born into, the traditions they were raised in, the social class they were part of, the bonds of religious belief they shared with others. Before the rise of the modern self, people simply inherited their identities, their "selves" directly from their families. The boy born to a shoemaker was destined to be a shoemaker. The girl born to an aristocrat would be a lady. But with the modern age came a new social mobility and with it the idea of the individual.

In my own case, my inheritance—the family and the world I was born into—left an array of possible choices before me. Neither of my parents had gone to college. My mother had gone to secretarial school and my father did one year of business school after high school before finding a fulfilling career in middle management. My oldest brother wasn't the academic type. He was six years older than me and upon graduating from high school had done a short stint at a logging school before enlisting in the U. S. Army in order to become an MP. My other brother was smart, a jock, and one of the most popular kids in school. He was on the fast track to college and successful yuppie-hood. He was also a goody two-shoes, and even though I was three years behind him in school, I'd already done more bad things than he would dream of doing in his whole life. If I was going to follow in anyone's footsteps, I had a whole range of tracks before me from which to choose. It made more sense to make my own way. What that way would look like—that was the question.

It's a question that could be asked only in the modern age. With such a question arose a literary form to give them voice: the novel. As a literary genre, the novel is, in fact, more than anything else about the rise of the modern individual, the creation of the self. As such, *Jane Eyre* is the quintessential story of the rise of the individual, the journey to create the self. The quest for self usually begins with the separation—first emotional, then physical—from one's parents. It is this long and arduous process of emotional separation, in fact, that we call adolescence. It was the process I was struggling through when I was chafing against my record-burning youth pastor, the nodding members of my church youth group, and my parents' expectation that I attend church with them each Sunday. This psychological feature of modern life explains why so many novels, from the form's very beginnings in the eighteenth century, have main characters who are orphans or foundlings.

Orphans are literally what all of us are metaphorically as we begin to try to define ourselves as individuals apart from our parents. Once we've done so, we spend the rest of our adolescence and young adulthood, hopefully, individuating ourselves from our friends and the rest of society. (In fact, it takes some people so long to do this that the process continues on into mid-life, which then manifests itself in the ubiquitous and notorious mid-life crisis.)

No longer gaining identity from the community, the modern individual stands not merely apart but in isolation. The modern individual is orphaned from the community of old; isolation—alienation—is in fact the modern condition.

Modernity is eighth grade stuck on "repeat."

This is why the first thing we learn about Pip in the opening scene of *Great Expectations* is that he is an orphan. Likewise, *Jane Eyre* begins with an orphaned young Jane describing a familial scene from the vantage point of an outside observer, an alien, despite her being right there in the room, for the fact of the matter is that in this family she is an outsider:

> Eliza, John, and Georgiana were now clustered round their mama in the drawing-room: she lay reclined on a sofa by the fireside, and with her darlings about her (for the time neither quarrelling nor crying) looked perfectly happy. Me, she had dispensed from joining the group; saying, 'She regretted to be under the necessity of keeping me at a distance; but that until she heard from Bessie, and could discover by her own observation, that I was endeavouring in good earnest to acquire a more sociable and childlike disposition, a more attractive and sprightly manner—something lighter, franker, more natural, as it were—she really must exclude me from privileges intended only for contented, happy, little children.'

Here Jane defines herself by not being a "contented, happy, little" child, by her exclusion from the family circle. Eliza, John, and Georgiana are merely her cousins, not her siblings, and their mother is to Jane only the cruel Aunt Reed, widow of her mother's late brother. Following this scene is Jane's cruel banishment to the frightful "red room"—the cavernous red chamber where Jane's Uncle Reed "breathed his last." This punishment is rendered for the act of defending herself against an attack by one of her cousins.

Although forcibly seized and taken to the room, little Jane— despite her helplessness on every level except the most inner and most personal—tells us, "I resisted all the way." This line is said by Joyce Carol Oates to be the theme of the novel, signifying as it does the pattern for Jane's life all the way to the end of the work. Despite the fact that she has no family in any real sense of the term, no means, no position, no love, and despite the fact that she longs more than anything for love and acceptance, Jane resists the tyranny of a world that tries to impose on her things that go against her true sense of self. In this way, Jane Eyre indeed reflects the state of the modern individual. In this way, Jane Eyre reflected me as I was trying to find my way to my self.

Excluded from all but the barest physical provision, orphaned from any community that could offer her a social or material inheritance as in the days of old, Jane has nothing from which to draw her identity. So she turns, like me, to books. The opening scene of the novel has Jane, scolded by her aunt, finding solace in reading Bewick's *History of British Birds* where she encounters environs much like her own state of isolation. She reads of "bleak shores," "forlorn regions of dreary space," and "firm fields of ice" where little birds like Jane might be found. But books offer Jane much more than mental escape. More importantly, they impart to her the gift of language, language skillfully used.

Language, throughout Jane's life, is the tool through which she creates and defends herself. This is why it is essential to the story of *Jane Eyre,* even though it is a fictional work, that it takes the form of an autobiography. Indeed one of the most distinguishing aspects of *Jane Eyre* is the "voice" of Jane. It is no coincidence that the term "voice" has come to mean in modern usage much more than just the sound made by the vocal organs, but also the means by which we make our individual selves known, not only to others but to ourselves. For the connection between the self and language is inseparable: it is through language that the self becomes.

Thus it is through language that Jane's process of becoming begins. Her first act of rebellion in the novel is to give voice to the thoughts and judgments she forms from her reading of books:

to pronounce her cruel cousin John Reed to be "like a murderer . . . like a slave-driver . . . like the Roman emperors!"—those other tyrants Jane had read about in Goldsmith's *History of Rome*. From this point on, throughout the short remainder of her stay with the Reeds, to her years at the Lowood orphanage, to her tumultuous connection with Edward Rochester, Jane exerts what little control she has as an otherwise politically and socially powerless woman of no means through her voice of sensitivity and longing and sharp wit. As she finds her voice, Jane's journey to selfhood is assisted by her resisting the natural temptation to become like the people whose love she desires but does not receive. She refuses to become like her cruel aunt or her tyrannical cousin John or her spoiled girl cousins. Yet, at the same time, like any little child, she wishes to be loved by them.

As it was for Jane, so it was for me. When The Group turned against me, I should not have been surprised. There is no tyranny like the tyranny of eighth-grade girls. They—we—were mean to everyone, with turned backs, sidelong glances, ferocious whispering, and, worst, long silences. I'm ashamed to say that until that meanness turned toward me, unlike Jane, I pretty much went along with them (despite my earlier kindness—and adherence to what was even then my truer nature—in sixth grade to Caroline). On the single occasion I was ever called to the principal's office, he told me that the girls' bathroom had been vandalized and that Caroline, the slow girl I had helped so much in sixth grade and had not been unkind to since, had reported seeing me do it. Of course, I had done no such thing, and the principal readily believed me.

I couldn't believe what Caroline had said about me. I hadn't even seen much of her since we'd all moved up into junior high and she'd been put in a special class. I couldn't understand why she would do this. But I think I understand now.

When Jane is removed by her aunt from Gateshead and taken to the charity school, Lowood, one of few comforts she finds within those cold walls is the friendship of her fellow inmate, Helen Burns. A strong Christian, Helen is able to transcend the misery of their surroundings, the sparse and often inedible food, the fever-inducing chill of their rooms, and the Pharisaical reign of Lowood's benefactor and master, Mr. Brocklehurst. Jane is attracted to Helen by her Christian virtues: her kindness, her patience, her perseverance, and her forgiving spirit; how Jane wishes for these, too! How wonderful to be able to escape through the power of the mind the pain of this physical world! Ultimately, the transcendence Jane sees Helen achieving proves to be the greatest temptation Jane has yet faced. But in a brief moment's contemplation of the small pleasures around her—the flowers, the dew, the moon—Jane has a moment of illumination. Despite the misery that has thus far comprised her short life, Jane realizes, "This world is pleasant—it would be dreary to be called from it, and to have to go, who knows where?" Jane has realized that for herself, despite her initial attraction to Helen Burns' otherworldliness, this world, even with its pain, its disappointments, its loneliness and despair, is made to be lived in and not risen above. This resolution steels Jane when she comes to face the prospect of living on in this world, even in horrible Lowood, when her beloved Helen is suddenly "called from it" by death and her soul is at last released to "who knows where."

I once faced, like Jane, ever briefly, the temptation to reject this world and all its goodness and pain. It was early one summer during Vacation Bible School at my family's little one room Baptist church plopped in the midst of pasture land on the south end of town. The day's speaker had talked about the rapture to the dozen or so of us kids of all ages filling the front pews. He talked about people disappearing in the air and cars and planes crashing and all the people left behind, but there was something else I couldn't stop thinking about. I wanted to cry, but I blinked hard so I wouldn't do so in front of everyone else. As soon as the preacher had stepped off the platform, pulling out a white handkerchief to wipe away the beads of sweat that had formed on his brow in the stifling air of the old church, and we kids were all being herded to the next activity, I ran down the church aisle, through the tiny foyer, and out the front door to sit on the big granite slab of a front step. It was early summer, which in Maine, when the sun is shining as it was that day, is pleasantly not hot.

The granite step I sat on was comfortingly warm, and the grasses all around me were richly green and smelled good. These things made me cry more. Within minutes my mother, who was also the VBS director, sat down beside me. She put her arms around me and asked me what was wrong.

"What about the horses?" I cried.

"What about them?" my mother asked.

"If we are Raptured, who will take care of them?" I wailed. I didn't want to go to heaven. I liked it here just fine. But even more importantly, I worried about what would happen to our pets, and to all the animals in the world, if the Rapture took place. My mother tried to console me as best she could, but didn't succeed. When we finally went home at the end of the day, I ran up to my room and cried as long and as hard as I think I've ever cried. I begged God as earnestly as I've begged him for anything just to take us all right then since I couldn't bear the weight of worrying about it any longer. Finally, tears depleted, I realized I was angry at God, mightily angry at him, for putting us—me—in this situation in the first place.

I can't say that this anger and sorrow were resolved in any sort of great epiphany. All I can say is that they dissolved eventually, by time, into acceptance. And much, much later, intellectual assent. But that was many years to come. Acceptance of the nature of God, the world, and others seems integrally connected to an acceptance of the nature of one's self, too. And this, I think, is where freedom, ultimately, is found. Freedom is not an endless sea of choices, but an acceptance, embrace even, of both the nature and the grace at the core of our being and our becoming—not the escape I begged God for so fervently that day in my room. I understand Jane's resistance to Helen's complete transcendence of earthly life, with both its joys and sorrows. For I, too, had once resisted the temptation of such an escape just as I had resisted, at least once, the temptation to be something I was not.

Jane's next temptation to betray her true self proves the most difficult of all and is the central event in the novel. Jane's love for her employer Edward Rochester—by all social and political measures her superior in every way—proves her soul to be more than the equal of his. Led to believe that Rochester intends to marry the beautiful socialite Blanche Ingram, Jane declares to Rochester her intentions to leave his home and employ rather than subject herself to the pain of seeing the one she loves allied to another. When Rochester protests her plans, she demands of him,

> "Do you think because I am poor, obscure, plain, and little, I am soulless and heartless? You think wrong!—I have as much soul as you, and full as much heart! And if God had gifted me with some beauty and much wealth, I should have made it as hard for you to leave me, as it is now for me to leave you. I am not talking to you now through the medium of custom, conventionalities, nor even of mortal flesh: it is my spirit that addresses your spirit; just as if both had passed through the grave, and we stood at God's feet, equal—as we are!"

Of course, Rochester does not have his heart set on Blanche Ingram at all, but on Jane. When he declares his love for her and makes plans to marry her, Jane experiences, for the first time in her life, a taste of happiness. Yet, as she tells her story from the vantage point of looking back, Jane realizes,

> My future husband was becoming to me my whole world; and more than the world: almost my hope of heaven. He stood between me and every thought of religion, as an eclipse intervenes between me and the broad sun. I could not, in those days, see God for His creature: of whom I had made an idol.

For Jane, such an idolization of anyone or anything above God was a betrayal of her true self. It took a great test of her religious faith, of being forced to choose between her love of God and her love of a man, before she could see what sacrifice would be re-

quired of her in order to remain true to her real nature. As anyone who has read the novel cannot forget, the only love Rochester
can offer Jane would require a betrayal of her convictions about
marriage based on her deeply-held Christian beliefs. This is a
choice she refuses. Despite some critics' assertions otherwise,
Jane's faith is real and not merely superficial. As Charlotte Brontë
explains in her preface to the novel,

> Conventionality is not morality. Self-righteousness
> is not religion. To attack the first is not to assail
> the last. To pluck the mask from the face of the
> Pharisee, is not to lift an impious hand to the
> Crown of Thorns.
>
> . . .
>
> These things and deeds are diametrically opposed:
> they are as distinct as is vice from virtue. Men too
> often confound them: they should not be con-
> founded: appearance should not be mistaken for
> truth; narrow human doctrines, that only tend to
> elate and magnify a few, should not be substituted
> for the world-redeeming creed of Christ. There
> is—I repeat it—a difference; and it is a good, and
> not a bad action to mark broadly and clearly the
> line of separation between them.

In other words, Brontë was attempting to depict a character that ad-
heres to the unchanging principles of her faith though she refused
conformity to the particular practices of her society. Doctrine and
practice, unfortunately, don't always neatly coincide.

At this point in the book, Jane—like me, an alien and pilgrim—demonstrates her possession of true freedom: the freedom
to be true to the self she knows she has been created to be.
She flees the temptation to live with Rochester without being his
wife not because she cares what others might think, but because
she cares what she thinks. She cares what her God thinks.
Jane cares little enough for convention that she'd have gladly de-

fied it if it didn't mean betraying her own genuinely held beliefs. Thus Jane makes the painful, nearly fatal, decision to be true to herself and to reject what she has every reason to believe will be her only chance for love with a true equal. Jane's faith goes beyond mere conformity to ritual and tradition to a rootedness in a relationship with her God that makes her religious belief authentic and real.

Yet, clearly, this is not an easy faith that offers comfort, solace, or shielding from difficult choices. It is all-too tempting for followers of any creed to seek shelter in the cave of convention, to resist risk, to march in line with fellow believers. Not Jane. Upon rejecting Rochester's offer to her to live with him as his mistress and departing from him, her answer when he asks her, despairingly, "What shall I do, Jane?" is "Do as I do: Trust in God and yourself."

It is not so easy, however, for Jane to follow her own advice. She is a person of strong convictions, but she is human, too. Like any woman would, she longs to be with the man she loves, and she fights with herself about her decision. She is a woman of faith, but it is a faith that denies neither the soul nor the body. Both have needs. Alone and friendless in the world, she wonders, who is there on earth to care if she does right or wrong? "Who in the world cares for you? or who will be injured by what you do?" she asks herself. Her inner dialogue continues:

> Still indomitable was the reply—'I care for myself. The more solitary the more friendless, the more unsustained I am, the more I will respect myself. I will keep the law given by God; sanctioned by man. I will hold to the principles received by me when I was sane, and not mad—as I am now. Laws and principles are not for the times when there is no temptation: they are for such moments as this, when body and soul rise in mutiny against their rigor; stringent are they; inviolate they shall be. If at my individual convenience I might break them, what would be their worth?'

During the years in which I was facing similar struggles in becoming my self—years that continued well past the eighth and ninth grades—I found in Jane an example of a young person who navigated that difficult middle way between the extremes of conventionality and safety, on the one hand, and rebellion and independence on the other.

It sounds so simple now, easy even, that act of eating lunch with a different group of girls, but it came out of the most hurtful experience I'd had in my short life. I know now that joining those girls and leaving the others behind changed the course of my life, placing me on the path toward teaching that Mr. Taylor had foreseen for me in the sixth grade. So it is that so much of our becoming comes not from within but from without, from the revelations others give us about ourselves, from beholding ourselves in the mirror held up in the world around us. "Beholding is becoming," as the philosopher Marshall McLuhan was known for saying.

But I didn't see all of that then. As it was for Jane Eyre, it was language—the power of my own voice—that helped me to get through it. I kept a journal, something I'd not done since keeping a tiny lock and key diary as a little girl. I wrote in it furiously, like Harriet the Spy, scratching into the wide-ruled pages of that orange spiral bound notebook all I was thinking about those mean girls and how foolish I'd been to play their games for so long. Funny how I remember so much more vividly what that notebook looked like than the words I wrote in it. It's like getting the words out not only erased the pain, but also the words themselves.

In so doing, I resisted the descent into what the school counselors called *low self-esteem*. Self-esteem is the dark, distorted shadow of self-possession. Self-esteem gazes inward and wills the inner eye to like what it sees; self-possession looks inward only long enough to take a measure then looks outward at the world in search of a fitting place—and settles for no less. Self-possession, although I certainly didn't know it then, is what made me refuse to grovel my way back into a circle in which I no longer fit.

But that doesn't mean it was easy. Stoic at school, I cried at home every day until one afternoon my mother and brother caught me, and I told them everything. My brother, who was three grades ahead of me at the same school, one of the most popular boys there, and who had never said anything nice to me in my life, spoke words I never will forget: "You're better than they are."

"I am?" I asked.

"Way better," he said.

I didn't cry anymore after that, and I began to enjoy even more my newfound friendships with the Smart Girls.

The words my brother had voiced became part of my voice, a voice that narrated the search for my self much as Jane's voice did in her search. Although the journal I kept during those chaotic days has long vanished into the past, Jane's story and her voice remain. It wasn't so much that I really thought, as my brother said in order to encourage me, that I thought I was "better" than those girls. What I came to understand is that in ceasing the futile attempt to be something I was not able or meant to be, and in striving to discover and be the person I was created to be, I would be a better self. The real disgrace was not in being kicked out of The Group, but in failing to fully embrace the grace that had made me who I was by trying to be something I was not.

A great deal of defining who we are as individuals is figuring out who we aren't. I wasn't what those popular girls were, but even more importantly I came to learn, I didn't need to be. When I didn't make the cheerleading squad in seventh grade, I decided to try cross-country instead. It was the sport my brother participated in to get in shape for basketball, his main sport. I wasn't that good at running at first, but by the time I was a junior in high school, I was one of the top three runners on the girls' team. We were state champions that year in Class D, the category for tiny schools like ours. In running, I discovered a life-long love, one that is an essential part of the self I have both discovered and cultivated. Such are the lessons of self-knowledge that Jane, and all of us, must learn.

I steered toward the middle less successfully than Jane did, however. In my own young life, the balance shifted toward nonconformity. Of course, conformity and nonconformity are meaningless terms apart from the things to which they are applied. In my case, I failed to conform, too often, to values and beliefs which, although instilled in me by my upbringing, were still genuinely mine. In betraying these, I betrayed myself. I mistook nonconformity for freedom and in so doing found myself anything but free. For it is in conformity to one's true nature that one is most becoming, in both senses of the word: well-fitted and beautiful.

Jane faces a similar temptation after running away from Rochester and his untenable choice. After nearly losing her life during her aimless journey to any place far from Rochester, she is eventually taken in and befriended by the Rivers family, consisting of two sisters and a brother, St. John.

St. John is a minister and soon-to-be missionary who asks Jane to join him in his missionary work as his wife. Jane has no disinclinations toward such a life or such a partner in work, but she will not allow herself to be joined in marriage to a soul that is incompatible with hers. For St. John does not want to marry Jane for love but rather for convenience. In fact, when he proposes to her, he says, "God and nature intended you for a missionary's wife. It is not personal but mental endowments they have given you: you are formed for labour, not for love. A missionary's wife you must—shall be. You shall be mine: I claim you—not for my pleasure, but for my Sovereign's service." (This is not a recommended model to follow when asking someone to marry you!) Although she would willingly accompany St. John as a Christian missionary, Jane explains that she cannot possibly go as his wife because their two "natures are at variance."

Ultimately, Jane tells St. John boldly, "I scorn your idea of love." Jane knows herself well enough to know that she possesses passion and feeling and a great capacity for love. She is indeed a woman, yet she is a woman who has spent most of her life alone and lonely and alienated.

Here at last is a decent man, one with whom she shares values if not passions, and once again, Jane struggles. "I felt veneration for St. John," she says, "veneration so strong that its impetus thrust me at once to the point I had so long shunned. I was tempted to cease struggling with him—to rush down the torrent of his will into the gulf of his existence, and there lose my own." There it is: The temptation, once again, is the same one Jane faced with Helen Burns and with Mr. Rochester, the temptation to betray her self, to surrender her own nature to someone else's.

This is the temptation I failed to overcome the first time I fell in love. Randy was, as they say, my high school sweetheart. He was the guy I couldn't look away from when I walked into the middle of Algebra on that first day at my new school, when my family moved from Maine to New York in the middle of my Junior year—and then couldn't look at when the teacher assigned me the seat near his. He was the guy that dominated every situation he was in. He was the guy that all the other girls in our crowd (and even some grown women) would have done anything to get. He was the guy I thought would never give me a second glance. But glance he did.

And more. Flattered, in love, I betrayed my faith, my values, my emotions, and my self-respect for a mess of pottage and a promise ring.

I should have seen it coming—algebra has never treated me right.

Like Jane, I turned Randy into an idol and for a while he—as Rochester for Jane—came between heaven and me. Randy told me what I should wear and what I should not. Who I could speak to and who I could not. When I wore more make-up than he liked to school, he sent me to the bathroom to wash it off. And I let him do these things. I betrayed my true nature and lost my self-possession. Ironically, despite the initial flattery of being pursued by someone like him, I never felt more unbecoming than when I was with Randy. Rather than being myself, I allowed him to recreate myself in his own image. I had not entirely learned the lesson of eighth grade; I had not entirely learned the lesson of *Jane Eyre*. But by reading and re-reading the story, eventually I would.

Some readers might find the means of Jane's resistance to her final temptation—that means being a supernatural call that brings her back to Rochester in a time and place where he can rightfully be hers—beyond belief. But such supernatural intervention is part of my belief because it is something I have experienced for myself. For me, as for Jane, that divine intervention brought the man who was right for me and allowed me to be true to my true self, as a woman, a Christian, and an individual.

Some readers find the ending, in which Jane is reunited with Rochester, but a weakened and crippled Rochester, a less-than-happy ending since Jane can become Rochester's "equal" only when he is in a diminished state. But the literal events in the story depict metaphorically the idea that a man who would treat a woman as his equal must sometimes be strong enough to let her be strong. Jane is ultimately united with a man who will not oppress her or overpower her but will let her be her self. I, too, ended up with such a man. Not, as in Jane's case, the first man I chose, but rather with a man I believe was of God's choosing and who, unlike the other man, was strong enough not only to let me be myself but also to encourage me first of all to discover who that self really was. Strong enough to let me be free to be the self I was created to be.

A pastor once said that even Christ's temptations—those he faced from Satan in the wilderness as well as those in the Garden of Gethsemane when he beseeched God for some other way than his impending crucifixion—were really temptations to not be true to his self, to betray his genuine nature and thus fail to fulfill the calling on his life. Even the greatest teacher who ever lived had to undertake the same journey for the self that we all do.

Ultimately, Jane Eyre succeeds in her quest to be the self—the person—truest to her nature. This is what makes her one of the first modern individuals in the history of English letters. No wonder one critic remarked in 1855, eight years after its publication, that "the most alarming revolution of modern times has followed the invasion of *Jane Eyre*." Jane Eyre is a revolutionary character because she chooses the integrity of her nature and self over social convention, material comfort, and even passionate love. She found true freedom.

In Jane I found a worthy role model on my journey to the freedom of becoming, fully and contentedly, myself. But before I could get to Jane, I had to take one, first tentative step. I had to walk into that classroom and have lunch.

6

The Only Thing Between Me and Tragedy:
Tess of the D'Urbervilles

All nature is but art, unknown to thee;
All chance, direction, which thou canst not see.

—from Alexander Pope, *Essay on Man*

It's hard to sleep sitting up on a train, even when the trip is days long and you are exhausted by lack of sleep, by loneliness, by fear, and by a tiny baby no one can see because he's tucked safely away inside your belly. The trip would be easier if you could afford a sleeper. But you have no money for such luxuries. The price of the one-way ticket took what little money you had. You're desperate for your last paycheck, a secretary's meager wages sent to the forwarding address. Years later you won't remember much about this ride. Was it four days long or five? What did you eat? How did you pay for it? All such details will vanish in the haze of time.

What you will remember most after all the ensuing years is the moment when the westward train burst through the Rocky Mountains and all you saw before you was an endless valley of dry, brown brush dusted by snow. You remember only this. And the wish that you didn't have to run so far so all alone—all the way from Boston to Seattle—but what else can you do? It's 1959. You are pregnant. You are unmarried. You are my mother.

A similar scene, decades earlier, is depicted by Thomas Hardy in his 1891 novel *Tess of the D'Urbervilles*. Here we find Tess Durbeyfield travelling by horse cart, pregnant and unmarried, afraid and ashamed, acquiescent. In this case, however, Tess is running not away from but back to her home—there were no trains then, no paychecks (no matter how small) for working girls, nothing to do but return home. And bear the double humiliation of being driven there by her rakish seducer, Alec D'Urbervilles.

The novel begins with Tess Durbeyfield as a young peasant girl whose father learns by chance that the family's ancestry is aristocratic. Emboldened by this useless piece of information, Tess's poor parents are able to convince Tess, aided by her feelings of guilt in accidentally causing the death of the family's horse, to call upon a wealthy family in a neighboring village, a family they believe, mistakenly, to be related to them through this ancient aristocratic line. Eventually, the outcome of this unlucky liaison is what would be called in today's terms the "date rape" of Tess by a member of this imposter family.

In narrating the events, Hardy purposely obscures the roles force, guile, and consent play during that fateful night in the forest between Tess and Alec Stokes-D'Urbervilles and in the months that follow. (In fact, the details of the rape scene were changed by Hardy himself in differing editions of the story, and in one version Alec drugs Tess.) What is clear is that Tess emerges as "maiden no more." Months later, she returns home and, months after that, she gives birth to a child. What is not so clear, at least not in the minds of Hardy's Victorian contemporaries, is whether or not Tess—despite no longer being a virgin—might still be considered pure. For Hardy the answer is clear, and the rest of the novel is the portrayal of this tension between what Hardy depicts as Tess's true state—purity—and the condition imposed upon her by what he viewed as the false values of her society.

In Hardy's view, Tess is an innocent victim. Moreover, her innocence has made her a victim. He insists on referring to Tess and his depiction of her as that of "a pure woman faithfully presented." Oh, what controversy these words provoked! In choosing the word "pure" to describe such a heroine—pregnant and unmarried—and writing in England in 1891, Hardy was calling into question not merely the definition of the word pure but also the values of the entire Victorian age.

Like Tess, my mother fled upon learning of her out-of-wedlock pregnancy, but away from home, not to it. She quit her job and, having virtually no money, took the train all the way across the country to the West coast home of a friend's mother— a woman my mother had never even met. Her fear of going home was not unfounded: when a cousin of hers had found herself in a similar situation my mother heard her own father—my grandfather—say that if that ever happened to one of his daughters, he'd disown her. My mother took him at his word.

A generation separated my mother and me, and more than that, plus an ocean, divided Hardy's world and mine. Purity was not merely unimportant in my world; it wasn't even a point of consideration. The chickens hatched in the sexual revolution of the 1960's were still coming home to roost, and these were the years before the backlash of the abstinence movement would set in. My mother taught me that sex should be saved for marriage, having learned this lesson the hardest way one can. But purity— whatever that meant—was not a topic under discussion at all—not in the classroom, not in the lunch room, not on *ABC's After School Special*, not in the late night whisperings during sleepovers with my friends.

To the contrary, most of my peers were fleeing purity in our Race Against Virginity. Even those of us who weren't quite ready to sign up for the race nevertheless diligently trained by trying to go just far enough, often enough, to maintain at least a certain amount of respect. This meant, beginning in seventh grade, games of Spin the Bottle and Seven Minutes in Heaven in darkened, music-filled basements and garages of homes where parents were allowed by mutual consent to present themselves only in ancillary areas; and make-out sessions during autumn hay rides put on by the Methodist church. They were faux hayrides, neither horse drawn nor on a hay wagon, but rather on the back of a flatbed truck loaded up with a few handfuls of hay and horny teenagers, driving around the streets of town while the minister stood with his back leaning against the truck cab, staring dully ahead for the duration of the ride, determined not to notice the shenanigans going on in the hay at his feet.

I learned firsthand what French kissing was in that hay, and it took me quite by surprise. Meanwhile, one of my friends in The

Group had gone to third base at one of those basement parties. By the end of eighth grade, my friends who were dating high school boys from other schools had—if they were to be believed, and I had no reason not to—gone all the way.

So by the time our tenth grade biology teacher passed around various birth control devices in class one day as part of a lesson on reproduction it was pretty much a case of locking the barn door after the horses had gotten out. One girl a couple of grades ahead was rumored to have had an abortion already. The first girl in my class to get pregnant, Peach Fuzz, did so the summer between tenth and eleventh grade, pretty certainly on purpose. This girl lived in a trailer with her mother, an abusive stepfather, and five siblings. She'd always said she wanted six kids of her own, and she seemed nonchalant about getting such an early start. I know I felt as she did, wrongly, that we were much more grown up than we really were. The thing that nagged at me most, in my inability then to see completely the gravity of her situation, was watching her eat Humpty Dumpty potato chips every day for lunch. That couldn't have been good for the baby, I thought.

We had all overcome the drama of my move in the eighth grade from The Group to the Smart Girls, and Peach Fuzz and I had developed a fairly easy camaraderie as two of the top runners on the girls' cross country team. On the first day of school that fall, our coach caught me walking alone outside the main building and approached me. His face was sort of twisted and one eyebrow was raised higher than the other. I was pretty sure I knew what was coming. "Is the rumor true?" he asked with concern.

"Which one?" I said coolly, as though I were so in the know that I knew everything that was going on. Which of course was ridiculous and I knew it. Now that I think about it, the coach probably knew it, too.

"Will one of our runners be out this season?" he asked.

"Yeah, it's true," I said. We both knew what we were talking about. No doubt about that. With Peach Fuzz off the team, I moved up a slot and became one of our top three runners.

Suffice it to say that in my world, purity seemed to be the farthest thing from anyone's mind, but the old books I read offered a different world. This chasm between my world and the various kinds of worlds I encountered in books was one of the things that kept me reading. The characters I read about in books seemed so much like people I might know, but so often the worlds they inhabited were utterly unlike my own. These differences helped me to see that the manners and mores of my times were not unchangeable, not unquestionable. The world of *Tess of the D'Urbervilles* offered just such a challenge.

In response to widespread criticism of his idea of purity after the novel's initial publication, Hardy declared defiantly that his "heroine was essentially pure – purer than many a so-called unsullied virgin: therefore I called her so." At the very least, as her beloved Angel Clare later puts it, no matter what Tess's own role was, she was "more sinned against than sinning." Angel is right, of course. The philandering Alec had victimized Tess. When Angel meets Tess long after that event and judges her to be the simple, unsullied child of nature he has been seeking in a wife, Tess's essential purity—her innocence—still shines through. But when the idealistic Angel learns that Tess is not a virgin, he no longer views her the same way. Although Angel has consciously rejected the traditional values of his parents and surrounding society, it seems that the progressive views he has adopted intellectually have not seeped into the core of his being: he is still bound to traditional views at heart. So in saying these words of assurance to Tess (and himself), Angel, a fictional reflection of the prevailing attitudes of the real people of Victorian England, doesn't truly believe them. Despite his best efforts toward more progressive views, the views of the society he is part of, but has tried pridefully to rise above, are too deeply ingrained to peel so easily away.

That perspective was rooted in a world in which the sexual double standard was as alive and well as ever it has been. For the Victorians, virtue and virginity were synonymous: a woman who lost her virginity outside of marriage—regardless of the circumstances surrounding that loss—was ruined. For all intents and purposes, a woman's virtue resided in her hymen. Will—a woman's will at least—played little or no part in the business. The Victorians, certainly not the first or the last to do so, had confused virginity, a physical state, with virtue, a metaphysical condition. Unlike virginity, virtue is located not in the hymen but in the soul: in one's spirit, one's desires, in one's thoughts, one's will. In Tess, the narrator reveals Angel's eventual understanding of this:

> . . . he now began to discredit the old appraise-
> ments of morality. He thought they wanted read-
> justing. Who was the moral man? Still more
> pertinently, who was the moral woman? The
> beauty or ugliness of a character lay not only in its
> achievements, but in its aims and impulses; its
> true history lay, not among things done, but
> among things willed.

The virtue of the soul is expressed through the willful acts of the body. It involves one's whole being and thus is not surrendered by means of brute force or by singular acts. This understanding is the basis for Hardy's insistence upon Tess's purity.

Hardy was a man ahead of his time. Today most would disagree, alongside Hardy, with the Victorians' reduction of a woman's virtue to her physical parts. Such a view was simply another example of the same compartmentalization depicted in the character of Wemmick in *Great Expectations*. For Hardy's contemporaries, his novel offered a challenge to this merely physical, compartmentalized, view of virtue and purity. Hardy's refusal to deem as impure a woman who was clearly a victim raised much controversy, controversy which showed just how necessary such a challenge was. The fact that most enlightened people today would not dream of viewing a victim of rape as impure simply because she was raped shows how far we have come toward a holistic view of the physical body and the individual will. Or have we?

Victims of these detestable acts continue to feel the way Angel made Tess feel—impure, guilty, and ashamed—because society does not teach them to feel otherwise. Could it be that in theory we have as a society achieved progress beyond the Victorianism of the Victorian age—but in personal practice we've perhaps not come so far?

I've been close to victims of rape, both male and female, close enough to know the pain they go through in feeling sullied, stained, and impure, in feeling like "damaged goods," despite the fact that what was done was done to them, not by them, and not in accordance to their will. It seems to me that these women and men need as much to be defended, to be "faithfully presented," to themselves—as Tess needed back in 1891, to her contemporaries. Times change, perhaps, but people less so.

One semester I assigned *Tess of the D'Urbervilles* to my freshman composition class at a women's college where I have taught occasionally. One of the students had trouble keeping up with her work from the beginning of the semester. My students were freshmen, so I wasn't overly concerned since they often have problems adjusting to college life during their first year. But when we started to read *Tess* in the latter part of the semester, she fell even further behind. I called her in for a conference in my office before class one morning. I made small talk with her for a few minutes before asking her about her work in the class.

She was a slight young woman with dark hair and nervous hands. The office—indeed the entire campus—had an Ivy League feel about it with gracious brick buildings and warm wooden floors and bookshelves and lushly upholstered furnishings. Such a traditional setting seemed incongruous with the stories I'd sometimes hear my students exchange about drunken parties and boyfriends sleeping over in the dorms. I could feel, on a smaller scale, this incongruity again with the girl's tapping fingers and the way her body seemed to shrink into itself when she talked. I wondered briefly if I had been this lacking in confidence when I was a freshman in college. When I asked her why she'd been missing class, she said she had stopped reading the novel after our first class discussion of it. In that class, we had talked about Tess's rape.

I asked her why she'd stopped reading, and she blurted out that she had been raped at her last school, which is why she had transferred here, and she didn't like students debating about whether or not Tess had been raped or seduced.

None of this was shocking to me, but, of course, I wanted not only to comfort the young woman but also to get her to see that talking about such an event in a book was a safe, constructive way of dealing with these issues. As she talked more, sharing few specifics but many hints, I could see that the ambiguity surrounding her rape was not entirely unlike Tess's. Like Tess, she had become pregnant but, she said, she "lost" the baby. I didn't dare ask what she meant by that. The way she said "lost" sounded like someone else's word, not hers, like a word someone else might have told her to use. She had transferred to this new school in hopes of a fresh start. Hearing her classmates carelessly bandy the word "rape" about during our passionate discussions of the book was unbearable for her.

I told her I was sorry about all she'd been through and was going through. By this time, we had finished discussing the book in class, and she felt confident that she could read it on her own and make up the assignments, which I agreed to. I didn't press the point with her, but I was dismayed that the lessons of those passionate discussions in class—Hardy's insistence upon Tess's purity—had not made a difference in the way this young woman thought about her own experience or herself. Although I know that what is true in fiction isn't always true in real life, I still somehow—as a teacher of literature and as a student of literature—want all of the lessons that can be learned from books to make an immediate transfer from the pages to the minds and lives of those who read them.

But they don't. The pages of books can change lives—as they have done mine—but it's not always so simple a transaction as merely reading the book and walking away, life transformed. It takes time for this to happen. If it happens at all.

Life, like a great book, is complicated. People, like the best fictional characters, are complex. Thus while Hardy takes great pains to establish the character of Tess as pure in the sense of being virtuous, he is just as careful to depict her as realistically complex. For this reason one critic has called Tess "that rare creature in literature: goodness made interesting." She is a poor peasant girl with aristocratic ancestry. She is innocent and childlike with a womanish appearance. She is spiritual without a rigorous adherence to religion. She seems at once a goddess and a child of nature. She is passionate but passive. She is a lot like my mother.

Human complexity is what makes understanding human beings, whether real or fictional, so difficult at times; empathy with
good but imperfect characters, or real people, isn't always easy.
This is why Hardy's contemporaries had trouble viewing Tess, as
Hardy did, as pure. Our prejudices, preferences, and ideals blind
us from seeing others as they are. In our blindness, we re-create
people—and even ourselves—in our own image, as Angel Clare
realizes, too late, he has done to Tess. After revealing her sexual
past to Angel, he recoils from her. She implores of him,

> 'I thought, Angel, that you loved me—me, my
> very self! If it is I you do love, O how can it be
> that you look and speak so? It frightens me! Hav-
> ing begun to love you, I love you for ever—in all
> changes, in all disgraces, because you are yourself.
> I ask no more. Then how can you, O my own
> husband, stop loving me?'
>
> 'I repeat, the woman I have been loving is not
> you.'
>
> 'But who?'
>
> 'Another woman in your shape.'

Angel has not been in love with Tess; Angel has been in love with
an ideal that he imagined Tess to be. This false image of Tess
blinds Angel to the real person Tess is, just as Hardy's contemporaries were blind to Tess's essential purity because of her circum-
stantial sullying. As Azar Nafisi explains in *Reading Lolita in Tehran,*
such blindness is "the most unforgivable crime in fiction."

"Evil," Nafisi writes, "in most great fiction, lies in the inability to 'see' others, hence to empathize with them. What is frightening is that this blindness can exist in the best of us...as well as
the worst."

Thus blindness—whether physical of metaphysical, literal or
metaphorical—is a recurring theme throughout literature across
the ages and genres. From Oedipus Rex, that archetypal tragic
hero, who exchanges his intellectual blindness to his true identity

as his father's murderer and his mother's husband for a self-in-
duced physical blindness, to the enfeebled and blinded Edward
Rochester at the end of *Jane Eyre,* to the absurd Hamm in Samuel
Beckett's play *Endgame,* the pages of great literature are filled with
figures who exemplify this quality that defines the human condition. Paul describes this blindness in the New Testament as
"see[ing] through a glass, darkly." No wonder so many of the physical healings performed by Jesus were those that restored sight:
such miracles serve as metaphors for the greater miracle that transforms us from ignorance to illumination. Jesus gave sight to the
blind, and in a much smaller way great books do, too.

Blindness is particularly significant in tragedy, and *Tess of the
D'Urbervilles* is a classic example. One of the essential ingredients
of tragedy in the classical understanding is that the tragic hero or
heroine, along with suffering great loss, gains insight and illumination. In other words, in undergoing the tragedy, the hero comes
to see the truth that has eluded him as Angel Clare does, albeit
too late for Tess. Hence the tragic end is not complete loss, for in
the process of loss knowledge is gained—by hero and reader.
Tragedy is then more than just a sad story; it is cathartic and en-
nobling. This is why Arthur Miller claims that tragedies are, ultimately, optimistic: "In them, and in them alone, lies the belief,"
Miller says, "in the perfectibility of man."

In this way tragedies hint at man's divine nature, the image of
God in us. Fittingly then, the process of gaining insight is often assisted by a religious prophet or seer. In classical tragedy this seer
is always blind: with a physical blindness that makes prophetic insight possible, the blind seer serves as a foil to the stubbornly un-
seeing hero. In *Tess of the D'Urbervilles,* Angel—a tragic hero—is
assisted in his enlightenment by a prophet in the form of an un-
named sojourner who accompanies Angel for a brief while during Angel's self-exile in Brazil. This prophet simply and "plainly"
tells Angel that "he was wrong" to leave Tess. This is the turning
point in Angel's long, slow journey to illumination. In tragedy,
though "seeing" comes, it comes too late for the tragic outcome
to be averted.

In the tragic mode, the race against time always finds time the victor; the tragic hero loses. The tragic view of life sees time as the enemy. In tragedy, as time closes in, it spirals inward toward inevitable doom. Thus in *Tess of the D'Urbervilles,* the time it takes Angel to come to the right understanding and action toward Tess and her past comes too late: "'Too late, too late' said she, her voice being so hard that it echoed in the room, her eye glittering unnaturally." For Tess, it is too late. The cost of Angel's delayed illumination about Tess—and his error in judgment of her—is her life.

Yet the tragic hero's fall is not entirely his or her own doing. As in life, it is more complicated than that. There is the role of fate, or, in Hardy's view, chance—those things that are beyond human control. There is simply the matter of the complexity of human beings and the human condition. Tess, as already seen, is such a complex character. Indeed the complicated sometimes contradictory qualities of her personality contribute to her tragic fall, qualities determined, as Hardy's omniscient narrator makes clear, by ancestry and fate, beyond human control. As a tragedy written in the classical vein, *Tess of the D'Urbervilles* depends upon this central role played by fate, or determinism in the terms of late Victorian England, irrevocably tainted by the materialist views of Charles Darwin. In returning to the classical model, this novel portrays a less modern idea of the self than seen in other novels of the age.

Rather than developing out of the modern ideas of the creation of the self as seen in *Jane Eyre,* Tess harkens back to more ancient ideas about the role of heredity. The most significant and cataclysmic aspects of Tess's personality are those not of her own making but those she has inherited. From her mother come her attractive face and voluptuous figure. From her father—and the entire D'Urbervilles line—come her latent pride and constitutional passiveness.

It is this trait in particular that is Tess's tragic flaw: her passivity, her sole inheritance from her ancient familial lineage. For under the old aristocratic system, wealth and privilege were the results of a literal passivity, being "passed on" though inheritance, rather than acquired through work or individual effort, the qualities that brought about modernity's rise of the individual. This is why the ambiguous circumstances surrounding that night in The Chase are not important to her status as rape victim: whether she was taken by Alec through force or through seduction, equipped by neither nature nor circumstances to do otherwise, she passively succumbs to this fate. This passivity is both literal and symbolic: literal within the story's plot and symbolic of her role as an archetypal tragic heroine victimized by a combination of her own choices and forces beyond her control. This is how Hardy could deem Tess as "pure" despite her "ruined" physical state: she does not will such a thing even as she does not know how to exert her will against it. Even Angel, in the midst of his slow journey to illumination, sees this role of determinism, telling Tess:

> 'I cannot help associating your decline as a family with this other fact—of your want of firmness. Decrepit families imply decrepit wills, decrepit conduct. Heaven, why did you give me a handle for despising you more by informing me of your descent! Here was I thinking you a new-sprung child of nature; there were you, the belated seedling of an effete aristocracy!'

In the world of Hardy's complex but perfectly constructed tragedy, Tess's flaw combines with the forces of chance to arrive at the inevitable tragic outcome. The accidents of chance are woven throughout the story from beginning to end.

Life is, of course, filled with such accidents, but generally they don't so neatly resolve into pure tragedy (or comedy), but into more complex outcomes with loose ends and various possibilities. In the real world, whatever power chance has to shape the course of events, its power can never overcome the power of human will to respond. But in the fictional world of the novel, Tess's essential goodness is foiled by the power of chance. The narrator sardonically asks of these events where God was when Tess was so cruelly treated:

But, might some say, where was Tess's guardian

angel? where was the providence of her simple
faith? Perhaps, like that other god of whom the
ironical Tishbite spoke, he was talking, or he was
pursuing, or he was in a journey, or he was sleeping and not to be awaked.

For Hardy—and thus for Tess—God is merely an idea, an absence, a wayfaring stranger.

Not so for me.

God was not on a journey on the night I had planned—I was
not as passive as Tess—to lose my virginity. No, he was there.
Literally. Well, not God himself, but his people. His representa-
tives. They actually knocked on the door—literally.

My parents had gone out of town for a few days. Randy and
I had planned for him to come over on Wednesday night. He had
been waiting remarkably patiently, I thought, for me to decide I
was ready to take the plunge. After all, he had tripped the light
fantastic when he was fourteen years old. I knew that he would be
prepared, as all the guys in school generally were, carrying protection in their wallets all the time, if less out of responsibility
than out of the desire to act as if they might have need for it at a
moment's notice, and the ability to flash the foil wrappers in their
wallets when paying for lunch at the school cafeteria. It was late
fall, so it got dark early, which was a good thing, since Randy was
driving his father's car and was expected back home with it by
nine.

I felt a little (okay, a lot) guilty because I knew the only reason
my parents would leave me on my own for a week was because
they thought they could trust me. On the other hand, if I was
making this decision, and being responsible enough to be safe,
then didn't that prove that I deserved to be trusted? I told myself
so, and tried not to think about the guilt while Randy and I laid
back on top of my twin bed with the dark blue comforter on it
that I had picked out myself. When we had moved into this house,
the entire Frank-Lloyd-Wright-suburban-knock-off needed re-
decorating. My parents let me pick out everything for my room,
even the carpet. Having had only my brothers' rooms as hand-me-

downs in our previous houses, I'd never had a room that I got to decorate and furnish entirely from scratch. And I'd never had new carpeting before. I chose blue. Everything in the room was blue.

It is said that the advice of the Victorians to newlywed wives upon fulfilling their marital obligations was to "lie back and think of England." Although I was far from Victorian—after all, I had chosen this, wanted this, and had turned down many other opportunities before this one in order to make my first time right according to my own chosen standards—I couldn't help but lie back and think about that blue comforter.

Suddenly, halfway to the promised land, I heard a noise from the other side of the house. It sounded like knocking. We stopped fumbling in the pitch darkness and listened. It was knocking. On the front door. Insistent knocking. My heart suddenly pounded. What it had been doing a few minutes before, clearly now, was not pounding, not like this, anyway. I grabbed my flannel shirt and buttoned it on my way to the kitchen, guided only by the small light that was on over the kitchen sink. The rest of the house was dark. Beyond the kitchen was the side door, where the knocking was becoming unbearably insistent. I reached the outside light switch and flicked it on as I looked out the storm door window. Encircled in a halo of light from the bulb overhead were Mr. and Mrs. Brownfield. From church. What were they doing here? I opened the door.

"Hi!" they said. "You were supposed to babysit tonight."

It was more of a question than a statement. What night was it, anyway? It was Wednesday! I was supposed to babysit for them while they went to a church meeting. Caught up in my plans for my own de-flowering, I had completely forgotten my babysitting commitment. I could feel heat rising from my chest to my face. I knew my hair was jumbled and wondered if my heavy black eye makeup was all over my face. I didn't dare look down, but I was pretty sure my shirt was buttoned wrong, too.

I said the first thing that came to mind, which wasn't exactly a lie: "I'm sorry. I'm not feeling that well, and I completely forgot."

They stood there looking at me. Then they finally said okay, and walked away. The circle of light on the porch was now empty, save a few small moths circling around. My heart was still racing, as was my mind. How could this be happening? Why were they both here? Who was watching the kids now? How could I have been so stupid to forget what night it was? Was this even real? Would they tell my parents? I closed the door, turned the outdoor light off again, and walked slowly back to my bedroom where Randy was waiting in the darkness.

Unlike Hardy's God, mine had been knocking on the door. But I didn't let him in.

I wish I could say that this divine intervention caused me to open my eyes, to change direction, to get back on the straight and narrow, to send Randy on his merry way, and to heed finally the warnings I'd heard all my life in church and from my mother. But I can't say that. If there was an aspect of fate that combined with my own tragic flaw here, perhaps it was the world I was born into, the one in which purity was given ne'er a thought. And my tragic flaw? Well, I guess it was that continued blindness to the real freedom that was always before me but which I kept mistaking for something else.

I continued on that course for quite some time, but I didn't forget about how God showed up that night. I wasn't very happy with God then—or for a long time—but I couldn't deny that he cared. That I was his. And when eventually Randy decided he no longer loved me, or at least not only me—despite going through with my plans later that night and many other nights—I remembered the God who demonstrated his love for me just by showing up. Not by chance.

Of course, "chance" is merely the name human beings assign to events whose cause is unknown to them. As an agnostic skeptic, Hardy did not believe in an unknown First Cause or Mover behind all events. In his worldview, all was merely the result of happenstance. But believers in a sovereign God know that there is no such thing as *chance* in the design of Providence. Human blindness to Providence does not mean there is no design. And often—not always, but more often than not—time removes man's blinders to reveal the design behind things that appear at first to have no rhyme or reason.

This redemptive element of time—the ability of time to reveal an unseen design and to achieve restoration—is part of a comic view of life. In the classical sense, comedy, tragedy's counterpart, didn't refer to a work that was funny or humorous, but simply one with a happy ending, usually a marriage. The loss and death of tragedy was counterbalanced by the promise of new life implicit in the idea of marriage. Yet, both tragedy and comedy result in illumination: the difference is that in tragedy, the illumination occurs too late for the course of events put in motion to be stayed; in comedy the illumination is the catalyst for a new course of action, such as the one I took long after the knock on my door that night. In tragedy, time closes in toward inevitability; in comedy, time opens up new possibilities. While tragedy and comedy offer different endings for their respective characters, they both offer lessons for their audiences.

All these ingredients of tragedy and comedy and of Hardy's tragic novel are, of course, the stuff of life—human exertion and human passivity, the forces of accident and chance, the destructive and restorative aspects of time. But there is one essential ingredient of life that is missing in the world Hardy depicts in *Tess of the D'Urbervilles,* and its lack is the ultimate cause of the tragic outcome. That missing element is grace.

Grace is an interesting word. It can mean *unmerited divine favor, help,* or *reprieve.* Or—*beauty, decorum,* and *elegance.* It might be difficult at first glance to see how *reprieve* and *beauty* go together, but further reflection suggests the first group of meanings centers on the cause while the second on the effect. Taken together, both clusters of meaning point to grace as the bestowal or possession of a pleasing, or even sanctified, state—a state pleasing to both possessor and beholder. To put it more simply, all the variations of meaning point, essentially, to goodness bestowed or gained, goodness in both a moral and an aesthetic sense.

Now, while these elements of grace are not entirely absent from Tess, the absence of grace at the story's core is what makes the story tragic. First, the world of this novel is a world without God. One set of definitions for grace involves divine assistance or reprieve. In *Tess of the D'Urbervilles,* God is not only absent, but

Hardy takes it one step more in linking religious belief with outdated pagan superstition, Victorian hypocrisy, and with the ob-
struction of justice. Further, the grace of empathy, compassion
and, ultimately, forgiveness is missing. In the novel, as in tragedy,
it is blindness that prevents such compassion. When one is blind,
as Angel is, to one's own inconsistencies or flaws, one is unable to
empathize with the human frailties in others and thus unable to
offer forgiveness. Divine grace is reflected in human acts of forgiveness. Forgiveness, by definition, is gratuitous, derived from grace,
or unmerited, undeserved. The tragedy of *Tess of the D'Urbervilles*
results from forgiveness withheld—or given too late.

The effects of this lack of forgiveness are woven throughout
the novel. The pivotal event of the entire story is the inability of
Tess's bridegroom, Angel Clare, to forgive Tess for the impurity
she confesses to him on their wedding night. It is at this point
when the culmination of all the events thus far will lead to redemption or destruction. Tess begs Angel,

> 'Forgive me as you are forgiven! I forgive YOU,
> Angel.'
>> 'You—yes, you do.'
>> 'But you do not forgive me?'
>> 'O Tess, forgiveness does not apply to the
> case! You were one person; now you are another.
> My God—how can forgiveness meet such a
> grotesque-prestidigitation as that!'
>> He paused, contemplating this definition;
> then suddenly broke into horrible laughter—as
> unnatural and ghastly as a laugh in hell.
>> 'Don't—don't! It kills me quite, that!' she
> shrieked. 'O have mercy upon me—have mercy!'
>> He did not answer . . .

Angel's refusal to forgive Tess—at least not until it is too late—sets
their lives on the inevitable path to destruction. But for grace—
forgiveness—how different it could have been! Of course, the fact
that it is not is what makes the novel the perfect tragedy that it is.

Yet, while grace is absent from the world within the novel, the novel's very existence comes through grace: that is, the grace offered by the author himself. In his depiction of a world without grace Hardy is demonstrating the very need for that grace. Even more, in his insistence on presenting Tess "faithfully" as a "pure woman," Hardy embodies the very grace he sees missing in his own society. In showing the tragic results of blindness and the failure to forgive, Hardy illustrates the power forgiveness has to avert tragedy. Furthermore, as in the classical tragedies, Hardy elicits for his character great pity, another form of grace, from the reader and thus creates from his story an attitude of grace, not in his fictional characters, but in us—real people in the real world in need of real grace.

I, for one, owe no less than my life to this same sort of grace that Hardy offers to Tess and asks of his readers.

More than half a century after Thomas Hardy published *Tess of the D'Urbervilles,* my young, unmarried mother gave birth to a son. Much like Tess a generation before and like most of the women of her generation, my mother had been raised in ignorance about sex. No wonder she was deliberate in raising me otherwise. This was partly the reason for my parents' open attitude toward books when I was growing up. This is also why my mother was very intentional about cultivating communication between us on every issue. The details leading to my mother's pregnancy are unimportant. But what is relevant begins with the fact that my mother was as innocent and ignorant as Tess in these matters: she was just as pure. But here the similarities end.

First, let us return to the novel. When, four months following her employment there, Tess leaves the home and employ of the Stokes-D'Urbervilles and returns to her parents, she asks Joan Durbeyfield:

> 'O mother, my mother!' cried the agonized girl, turning passionately upon her parent as if her poor heart would break. 'How could I be expected to know? I was a child when I left this house four months ago. Why didn't you tell me

there was danger in men-folk? Why didn't you warn me? Ladies know what to fend hands against, because they read novels that tell them of these tricks; but I never had the chance o' learning in that way, and you did not help me!'

I imagine my mother wondering the same things of her mother— but not daring to voice such questions. In some ways, the poor, rural communities of the 1950's, like the tiny Maine town in which my mother was raised, were more Victorian than the Victorians. And when my mother learned of her pregnancy, she did not return home as Tess did. In fact, she did just the opposite: she ran as far away as she possibly could. When she had found herself pregnant, she was living away from home, in Boston, where she had landed a good job at Polaroid after finishing secretarial school. When she left, she told everyone that she had gone to the West Coast to work. But my grandmother, with a motherly instinct of her own, figured things out after a while.

And this is the part of the story where grace enters in.

Once my grandmother had figured out what was really going on, my grandparents packed up their car and drove across the country to find their daughter: to be with her for the birth of her child—their first grandchild—and to bring them both home.

To understand the magnitude of my grandparents' actions you need to know a bit more about them. For twenty-three years, since the year my mother was born, my grandparents had lived off the land of their Maine farm. Theirs was not the industrial, commercial farming so common today. Theirs was subsistence-level farming: a dozen or so cows that produced enough milk and butter for the family along with a little cash, enough pasture to provide hay for those cows, soil that grew cucumbers, potatoes, squash and whatever else the deer might leave alone, and 140 acres that produced wood to heat the home my grandfather had built. It was enough, barely. My grandmother gave birth to both of her children at home. The dresses the girls wore to their one room schoolhouse were made by my grandmother from the flowered sacks the grain for the livestock came in. There wasn't any hired farm help, just the two young daughters who worked alongside my grand-parents in the barn and fields, offering whatever strength their lit-tle sun-browned arms could muster. The money brought in from their roadside vegetable stand, augmented by the cash from my grandfather's weekend gigs playing the trombone at the local dance halls, was allocated for necessities such as clothes, fuel, and farm equipment—not cross country road trips and illegitimate children. So in addition to the moral ones, there were very real financial and practical obstacles for my grandparents to overcome in pursuing—in forgiving—their wayward daughter. But when abstract ideals were confounded by life, and when blind fear of the unknown was overcome by the known, grace—the highest form of love—stepped into the gap.

My grandparents drove to the West Coast, found my mother, and stayed with her for the birth of her child. My grandmother urged my mother, "Come home, where people know you," rather than start all over among strangers. And so she did. There she found the grace that can exist even in small, rural towns of the 1950's.

My grandparents took my mother back to the family farm where they all lived together until my mother met and married my father, and they formed a family of their own, one which eventu-ally included me. The illegitimate child that the delivering doctor urged my mother to give up for adoption is my oldest brother. This—the sacrifice of my grandparents—is what makes the grace—the forgiveness—offered to their daughter, and, by exten-sion, their first grandchild, even more remarkable than grace by its very nature always is.

So it is literally to the grace of my grandparents that I owe the existence of my family and myself. It is grace that stood between my mother and a tragic outcome like that of Tess in *Tess of the D'Urbervilles*. And between me and the foolish mistakes I had made and continued to make. Indeed, the only thing that stands between me—or anyone—and tragedy is grace. For even as Hardy insists in the novel upon Tess's essential goodness, in a fallen world, goodness without grace is insufficient. This is why one critic called the story "a parable of the tragedy of a life without Christ."

So I take every unplanned pregnancy personally. For one thing, I know that there but for the grace of God, go I. But even more, every time I encounter or hear of a woman in such a situation—especially if she is young, and scared, and feels alone—I think of my mother, I think of her on that train, scared and alone, and I hurt inside. I want to comfort her and tell her that through the grace of God and people, it can be all right. Indeed it might even be more than all right.

With grace, the march of time offers redemption: lost opportunities do not mean that all is lost; grave mistakes can be transformed into blessings over time. It is never too late for God to come knocking on your door. This redemptive movement of time is part of a comic view of life, rather than a tragic view. It is a biblical view of time, one that sees time as moving in a linear progression toward an eternity which will subsume the temporary ravages of time. Time in its natural state marches steadily toward death and decay, but with the intervention of grace, time, along with human errors and lost chances, is redeemed. With grace, the tragedy of life is transformed into a comedy, a divine comedy. With grace, the pure in heart—like my mother—see God. And so do I.

7

Sex, Symbol, and Satire: *Gulliver's Travels*

No man is an island, entire of itself; every man
is a piece of the continent, a part of the
main....

—from John Donne, *Meditation 17*

I could barely see the stage from my seat in the nose-bleed section
of Buffalo's Memorial Auditorium. The smoke from fog machines
and joints only made the visibility worse. I was so high I couldn't
stand. I slouched back in my seat, squinting through the haze at the
Lilliputian performers below.

For heavy metal fans, this was the concert of the year, maybe
even the decade: double-headliners, Iron Maiden and Judas Priest.
My brain felt thicker than the air around me until I saw something
far below on the stage that jolted me out of my stupor. I leaned
forward, eyes narrowing. I asked someone nearby if I could borrow his binoculars and looked through them. Yes, I was seeing exactly what I had thought I was seeing: two barely-clad female
back-up singers, requisite for any heavy metal concert, were on-
stage performing in cages. I returned the binoculars to their owner
and sat back again in my seat and glared at the stage. All I remember of that night from that point on is sitting there and stew-
ing about those women in cages.

Of course, it was all part of the act. The women weren't actually trapped in the cages; they were there by choice, by their own
free will, and probably paid well for it. So why did it make me wish
I could feel the total weight of my anger, dulled as it was by a high
from which I tried in vain to shake free? But I'd willingly surrendered my freedom, no less so than those women in the cages.

If I had actually listened (really listened) to the songs played by these bands I would not have been so surprised. Had I paid attention to the lifestyle and worldview they promoted and not simply dismissed it as art, as though the art one makes has nothing to do with one's life, I'd have expected this. Had I paid attention to the jokes, the stories, the views, the behavior of the friends I'd come to the concert with, including my own boyfriend, Randy, I might not have been so surprised.

Not that there hadn't been nagging hints from time to time. Randy once told a writer for the school newspaper that what he wanted most for Christmas was a centerfold model, and reassured me after I objected that he was just kidding. When his friend said he'd never date a virgin, everyone standing around laughed approvingly. When another friend said he'd dig having two women at once, all the other guys agreed. I must have been listening because I still remember these things now, but I was foolish enough, naïve enough, to push away my concerns and tell myself *boys will be boys*. Besides, I actually believed Randy when he declared that it was different—he was different—with me. I didn't know that history is rife with women and girls who naively believe in the inverse of the fairy tales in which the knight in shining armor saves the damsel in distress—the myth that we can rescue a boy or man from his own wretchedness, foolishly—and pridefuly—thinking *with me it will be different.*

But I was no different. I settled for too little. Far too little.

I wish I could tell you things were different with me, with Randy, but they weren't. There really is no big story here. Just an embarrassingly trite cliché: The Girl meets The Guy, The Girl and The Guy fall in love, then The Guy meets Another Girl. In fact, as awful as it was at the time, I sort of knew in the back of my mind—from having read so many books—what was likely to happen. After all, The Guy had taken up with me in the first place while seeking advice on how to break up with the girl he was with at the time. Patterns repeat. I was smart enough to know that, even if I tried to pretend for a while, like many girls do, that I would be the exception to the rule. Call it self-fulfilling prophecy, call it poetic justice, call it what you will. My literary mind helped me recognize and appreciate—even beneath the piercing pain—such irony when I saw and lived it.

I had gotten pretty good at this ability to believe that the way one thinks or acts in one area of life doesn't affect other areas. I had not yet learned that the particular can't be separated from the general. Inner belief is reflected by outward expression. You can't disrespect or devalue one woman as a woman without disrespecting or devaluing them all. You can't uphold one standard of sexual ethics in theory and not have it affect your actual relationships. Those women dancing in cages were simply the logical extension of the values of the lifestyle my friends and I were living. Seeing those women that way that night cracked the façade of denial I had put in place over the years.

It was just a small crack at first. I still thought it was religion, the church, that wanted to put us all in cages. I still thought, or wanted to think, that this—the debauchery of a night like this with my friends at Memorial Auditorium—was freeing, this life of sex-and-drugs-and-rock-and-roll that I was dabbling in. It was quite a package deal, all of it a rebellion against the beliefs I thought I could hold to inwardly while behaving outwardly in contrary ways.

And I was living this way for no reason other than because I could. I wasn't troubled or depressed or abused or having problems at home or at school, or anywhere, really. On the other hand, most of the kids I was hanging out with had excuses I didn't have: divorced parents, alcoholic mothers, abusive fathers, dysfunctional families, and certainly a lack of religious upbringing of any kind. I'm not even sure they had actually consciously chosen this lifestyle. But I had. I knew better. From the start I'd been playing the game with a sort of double-mindedness. I knew I wasn't going to lead this sort of life forever. My best friend Rachael—one of the Smart Girls I'd been hanging around with since getting kicked out of The Group—and I would even joke about it. Were we someday going to be grannies sitting on our porch rockers, smoking up? We laughed at the thought because deep down, we knew we wouldn't be.

We had been raised with loftier, more traditional, ideas about the good life, but we were having a ball for the time being. We didn't want to stop, didn't need to stop, and couldn't see why we'd want to stop, at least not anytime soon. Yet, all around us Rachael and I saw people who had never stopped, never grown up or out of it, and weren't living any kind of good life. I knew, even though I didn't want to right then, that someday I'd grow up and lead a responsible and productive life, just as was expected of me by just about everyone. Just as I expected of myself. I could see a different future. I just couldn't see the bridge that would take me from here to there. Perhaps it wouldn't be a bridge that would take me, but a cage.

Those women in cages were a powerful symbol.

The first crack in this cobbled veneer I wore began when I saw myself recoiling at the symbol but not the reality the symbol represented. This life of reckless, carefree irresponsibility being celebrated on the stage and in these seats wasn't going to set anyone free. It would only enslave us, was enslaving us, no less than those cages. What kind of divided life was I living in which I could accept a lifestyle based on certain views but was insulted by its symbols?

Symbols are powerful. And we live in a symbol-saturated society. The power of symbols comes from the reality they represent. Very few of our experiences are unmediated by the symbols of an experience that enter our consciousness long before the actual experience. We see ads touting the smiles toothpaste will bring us before we have all our teeth. We watch commercials showing how much fun we'll have if we drink a certain brand of beer before we've lost the joy of blowing bubbles. We hear songs about romantic love before we have our first crush. Before we've even reached puberty, we watch sex as it is portrayed in the movies and television, imagine it as it is described in books, and laugh about it from jokes whispered by schoolmates. It's hard to imagine things otherwise.

But symbols are tricky. Some symbols are true and some are false. And there is probably no matter surrounded by more false symbols than sex.

I had yet to learn that everything I needed to know about sex I could have learned from a celibate, eighteenth-century, Anglican priest named Jonathan Swift. Swift not only understood sex, but he understood, too, the power of symbols and the importance of community, and how both of these are as much a part of what it means to be fully human as sex is.

Swift's most recognizable, most widely-read and widely-adapted work is *Gulliver's Travels,* a work so rife with symbols that it's allegorical at times. *Gulliver's Travels* seems to be simply a far-fetched and far-flung adventure tale of one Lemuel Gulliver (gullible as gullible can be) travelling to various lands of strange in-habitants—tiny people, big people, silly scientists, and the horse people—easily adaptable into a children's story, the book is much more than what it appears to be on the surface.

Swift crafted a serious satire targeting a melee of universal human problems and themes, as well as people and trends of his day, all worthy of extensive footnotes in the scholarly editions. But both in and beyond the satire, *Gulliver's Travels* reflects the holistic worldview of its author, a man who could see how one idea ripples toward another, how one false notion can lead to disastrous consequences, and how one aspect of human experience touches the whole. So while the lessons about sex—or, more properly, human sexuality—in *Gulliver's Travels* are not the most obvious ones, when they are seen in relationship to everything else in the work and in the body of Swift's work—indeed, for Swift, relationship was the key—they are profound.

That might seem strange given that not only are the references to sex in *Gulliver's Travels* few and far between but also that those few are rather crude. In fact, some critics (particularly later ones who viewed Swift through a more conservative, Victorian lens) accused his works of obscenity. It's true: the crudities are often a bit shocking to readers today who harbor the illusion that attitudes about sex have steadily coarsened over time. But the fact is that a chart tracing sexual mores over the trajectory of human history would look more like a roller coaster than a slide. No wonder those whose exposure to *Gulliver's Travels* is limited to the children's book or the cartoon adaptations are sometimes scandalized upon reading the complete, unsanitized edition.

For example, the children's versions usually include the memorable scene of Gulliver standing "like a colossus" while the Lilliputian army marches beneath him. But what is omitted is Gulliver's sly observation that despite the King's express order...

> ... that every soldier in his march should observe the strictest decency, with regard to my person; which, however, could not prevent some of the younger officers from turning up their eyes as they passed under me. And, to confess the truth, my breeches were at that time in so ill a condition, that they afforded some opportunities for laughter and admiration.

Centuries before Freud theorized about penis envy, the clever Swift presented his own version. Theories come and go, but human nature doesn't change.

Speaking of penises, it often takes a bit of delicate explanation from me to help my college students understand the irony in Gulliver's naïve and needless insistence to his readers that the rumors circulating about an illicit affair between him and a certain (very tiny) Lilliputian lady are utterly untrue. The children's versions also omit or alter the scene of Gulliver putting out a fire in the Lilliputian palace. He does so in the original book by urinating on it; her majesty, like the children's book editors, is none too fond of this turn of events. Furthermore, most of these children's versions leave the rest of the voyages out altogether. After leaving Lilliput, Gulliver's next voyage finds him in a role reversal: Gulliver is of Lilliputian size among the giants of Brobdingnag. Among many frightful, awkward, and humiliating experiences in this situation, a most uncomfortable scene occurs when Gulliver describes the things the ladies in waiting do to him and with him in the privacy of their dressing rooms. By the time we reach Voyage Four and the land of intelligent, talking horses called Houyhnhnms and hairy, goatlike humans called Yahoos, the near-attack on Gulliver by a detestable female Yahoo frenzied with sexual desire for him seems tame by comparison.

Swift's doctrine and faith, unlike that of some of his fellow clergymen in the Established Church, was the real deal. Thus despite his deep disappointment at being ferried away by political appointment to the nether island of Ireland, Swift truly ministered to the people there, becoming their champion and leader in their fight against the tyranny of the English throne. Despite his coarse humor, his harsh satire, and his seemingly bitter view of humankind, Swift's religious and moral beliefs were as authentic as any hipster believer today would want them to be.

Furthermore, Swift knew a thing or two about human nature and over-reliance on rationalism. Writing during the Age of Enlightenment, also known as the Age of Reason, Jonathan Swift was a British subject, a brilliant satirist, Dean of St. Patrick's in Dublin, and an advocate of the oppressed Irish. As a Christian and an Anglican minister, Swift viewed the error of putting too much faith in human intellect as merely a variation on the age-old problem of pride. He knew, too, that the collective wisdom of the ancients offered far more insight than could the new-fangled cult of the modern individual, a concept on a rapid rise during Swift's lifetime.

If any age in history had ample reason to take pride in the accomplishments achieved by individuals through the exercise of human reason it was this one, the late seventeenth and early eighteenth century. This was, after all, the age of Sir Isaac Newton's law of gravity and Rene Descartes's dictum, "I think, therefore I am," the age that saw the founding of London's Royal Society of London for Improving Natural Knowledge and the publication of the dictionaries and encyclopedias that made portable all human knowledge, the era of the newly-invented telescope and microscope, the discovery of the circulation of blood and the speed of light. It's easy to see how folks got a bit prideful and prone to putting too much stock in human progress—and not enough in things eternal and universal.

Swift played a role akin to that of the Old Testament prophets in pointing out the folly of his contemporaries' worship before the twin temples of rationalism and individualism. But rather than using the voice of doom and gloom, Swift provoked change by evoking laughter.

One of Swift's most famous works is *A Modest Proposal,* an unforgettable piece which satirically proposes that the Irish poor raise and sell their children to the English to eat. It's a shocking piece that many a reader from Swift's day to ours has, mistakenly, taken literally. But once it's understood that Swift's clever technique is to inverse the relationship of the symbol and the symbolized by depicting in literal fashion (the English devouring the Irish) what is happening symbolically (the English "devouring" the Irish through their oppressive policies), we have a key to understanding Swift's brilliance.

Bathroom humor, sexual innuendo, and the eating of infants are not what readers today expect from the works of quaint old writers from the eighteenth century, particularly if the writer is a clergyman, and an orthodox Anglican one at that. How is it that I consider Swift a trustworthy teacher of sound sexual morality?

It helps to situate Swift in his time: the England of the early eighteenth century was Christian in name, but religion was largely a lukewarm affair, making someone like Swift stand out even in his own time. For both religious and social reasons, morals and manners took cruder forms during this time than most today would expect. Marriages, for example, were undertaken for political and economic expediency, not love. And when we consider that London's "modern" sewage system allowed human excrement to run alongside the streets (even flooding over with too much rain, as Swift reminds us in one of his poems), we can grasp how less squeamish, by sheer necessity of exposure, the sensibilities of Swift and his contemporaries were regarding bodily functions of any kind. It's a bit easier to understand Swift's relatively conservative morality in the context of his culture, where his inverted symbols come into relief.

Our culture has inverted the symbol and the symbolized, too—but not in a move of sophisticated irony as in Swift. Rather, our cultural inversion catches us unaware. All around us semblances and simulations replace the real, sometimes to the point, it seems, that we no longer know the difference between the symbol and the symbolized. The inversion of symbol and symbolized is rendered complete when, for example, a symbolic experience such as porn replaces the actual experience. Of course, culture is so saturated with the symbols of sex, both true symbols and false, that the idea of actually experiencing sex in an unmediated, Edenic way is, although enticing, ultimately impossible to imagine fully. The movie *The Blue Lagoon,* which came out when I was a teenager, centers on a shipwrecked girl and boy who grow up in an island paradise apart from society and discover sex on their own. Yet, try as they did, the creators of the film couldn't imagine sex un-accompanied by symbols, for the story includes the children's discovery of erotic pictures in the wreckage that came ashore with them.

Most of us have numerous formative experiences that distort our understanding of sex through false symbols, just as this film demonstrates. Like the shipwrecked boy and girl, I, too, received an inadvertent sex education through erotica. Once, in seventh grade, I was at Farrah Hair's house on the lake down the road from my home. I lived in an old farmhouse that meandered, the way New England homes do, with a series of barns and sheds attached to the house in accommodation of bitter cold winters, and screen doors that opened out onto a long porch that looked out across a cow pasture. Farrah Hair, however, lived in a square-shaped mod-ern lake house with sliding doors that opened onto a deck jutting over the lake where she and her family spent the summer boating, swimming, and water skiing. I loved my farmhouse home. But I was fascinated by my friend's home and her family. Farrah Hair had confided in me her family's secret that her parents had fallen in love while they were both married to other people; eventually, they divorced and married each other. I didn't approve of this, but it still seemed strange and exotic to me in the same way their house with its sliding glass doors was. Her parents were out for a while that day and we were playing in their bedroom where we discov-ered a stash of dirty magazines under their bed. I'd never seen such magazines that close, only hints of them here and there from behind brown wrappers at the drugstore in the next town over (our town being too small for a drugstore). We passed the entire afternoon flipping through the thick, glossy pages, reading the most outrageous passages to one another, exchanging shocking pictures, laughing, and gasping. However, months later, at our next opportunity for an encore performance, we found that the magazines had disappeared and never a word was said about them.

No, not since Adam bedded Eve before the Fall has there been pure sex, unmediated by the symbols, suggestions, and shadows obscuring its true meaning.

Because sex is the bed of society, the place from which we all come, it is a community affair. For sex is not only about self but about the Other, too; and it is not only about the Other, but it is, ultimately, about all other people. Sex is about the human family. That's why marriage—in essence the societal stamp of approval on sexual relations—requires witnesses, a government license, and an official to perform it. Though most today would like to think otherwise, all of society is affected by the sexual union of two people. A symbol of sex that communicates something other than this reality is flawed. It leads to bondage, a cage like the ones in which those women danced, an unseen cage, but no less real. It leads to the simulation of sex replacing the real thing, which has been called "the death of sex." As I encountered the false symbols all around me, I recognized at some level that each one reflected the inevitable failures of do-it-yourself sexual morality.

Yet my own sexual morality was based on nothing more than this. Despite being in my sexual beliefs and practices what I viewed as more conservative, more thoughtful, and more moral than many of those around me, my sexual code differed only in degree from the standards of those of the people in those magazines, but it did not differ in kind. Do-it-yourself is do-it-yourself, regardless of the form it takes.

Clearly, I had made errors. Chief among them was my overreliance on the power of rationalization, not to mention my miscalculations about human nature. This is exactly why I needed the lessons of Jonathan Swift.

Before I met Swift, I had my mother, of course. She taught me a lot about the essence of sex. She made it clear my whole life that I could ask her anything about anything. And I did. Sometimes she might have thought it necessary to put my questions off for a while—like the time when I was about six and we had a house full of boys, my brothers' friends, and I saw an ad in a magazine for tampons. I'd seen the same powder blue cylindrical plastic case as in the ad in my mother's purse, but I didn't know what it was, so I asked her, and she said, "I'll tell you later." Another time some years later when I was riding in the car with my parents and the radio aired a news report about a Capitol Hill sex scandal, I asked them, "What's oral sex?" My mother said, "I don't think you're old enough to know about that just yet," so I waited about a year and asked her again, and she told me—but she always answered my questions.

She also told me about things from her personal experiences, like the mistakes she made. The mistakes she didn't want me to make. And I was glad I had a mother who talked to me about such things, about all things. Most of my friends didn't have such parents.

Even as a young person, I was more of an intellectual learner than an experiential one. I made decisions based on my thinking more than my feelings. Besides, I had the vicarious experiences gained from reading many books to draw on. I learned a lot from the lives lived on the pages of books. Of course, none of this guaranteed that my thinking was right, necessarily, but I tried to figure things out the correct way and to act accordingly, even if my reasoning was flawed or, even more likely, if I lacked sufficient information (experience, perhaps?) to draw sound conclusions.

So, armed with the lessons gleaned from my mother and from many books, and both the knowledge and the means to minimize the risk of making my mother's exact mistakes all over again, and with reasoned out values and views about sex of my own design, I proceeded according to plan. The plan was this: I would avoid my mother's mistakes—I would not be innocent or naïve and I would not get pregnant outside of marriage—and I would save sex (unlike many of my peers) for when I was in love.

I succeeded in avoiding my mother's mistakes.

But I did not avoid the essential error.

To begin with, there were a few holes in my plan.

For one: if I'd never been in love before, how would I know when I really was?

I mean, I'd had crushes on boys since grade school, but I knew, through reasoning, that such wasn't love. By the sixth grade I had used that always-busy mind of mine to figure out a pretty reliable test of love: I recognized, intellectually, if not emotionally, that if one was married to or in love with someone, that person would be the most important thing on earth. Ergo, if I were truly in love with someone, that person would be more important to me than my horse. Hence, the horse test: any time I had a crush on a boy I would ask myself if I would willingly give up my horse for the boy. As long as the answer was "no," then I knew it couldn't possibly be love.

Of course, I knew full well the standard for sexual morality taught within my Christian belief system. I knew that standard stood starkly against many of the symbols of sex that surrounded me everywhere. And I certainly understood the logic of that standard and the kind of freedom it tended to promote. But, even though math was never my strongest subject, I knew, too, that there is usually more than one way to solve for x. I chose to reject the formula of my faith in favor of what I thought was a reasonable facsimile. I chose to reject the accumulated wisdom of a community formed over centuries for my own momentary and individual decree. I decided love would be my standard for sex. I'd established the horse test, in order not to mistake a passing fancy for the real thing. And so I waited.

Sure, there were a couple of close calls—some weekend parties where things got a little out of control; a boyfriend in tenth grade that I thought maybe was my first love but realized just in time was not—but I always put the brakes on. I waited for love. I waited for The Guy.

The plan would have gone without a hitch. If it had been up to me alone, that is.

But, as I've already pointed out, I had forgotten about one important factor: the Other. Even the most straightforward math solution is bound to fail if just one variable is overlooked. And who knows? There may have been another variable in the formula, too. Remember how God showed up at my front door the night I had planned to lose my virginity? Yes, the same God I shooed away and shut the door on. Well, I believe in a God who not only intervenes in human affairs—again and again—but one who also makes banquets out of stale bread.

Unlike my own youthful, misguided notions, Swift's orthodox theology led him to a realistic understanding that all of man is fallen, and this includes man's reason. Reason, rooted in the mind of the individual, hearkens less, if at all, to the voice of communal wisdom. Communal wisdom, on the other hand, is tried and tested over time in ways that consider but transcend mere individual experience. One pet school of thinking in Swift's day that was overly individualistic was rationalism, the belief that truth can be discovered by reason alone. The more trust Swift's contemporaries put into rationalism, the more clearly Swift heard his call to correct the error. His method was to expose the errors of rationalism by taking it to its logical extreme. Thus in *A Modest Proposal,* the fictional persona offering the proposal gives a flawless rationale for his plan for the Irish to raise children for the English to eat. There is not a hole anywhere in the reasoning. The only thing the proposer leaves out is, well, everything else that makes us human: love, compassion, kindness, care, common decency, and the divine image in us.

Swift took all of those things seriously, and with them, the human condition, human nature, and human sexuality. His harsh satire, his bitter reproaches, and the "fierce indignation" that "lacerate[d] his heart" (as his epitaph states) were rooted in a high view of both God and humankind.

When I studied Swift for the first time and learned these things about him, I remembered myself in eighth grade, being chastised for taking things too seriously, for holding too high a view of things my peers joked about, for being a bit more reluctant to participate in the musical chairs of sexual experimentation. Even in that recognition, however, I see now how flimsy my seriousness was, blinded as I was for so long to the fact that a foundation stronger than myself was the real, although unacknowledged, source of my seriousness. I needed something more than myself to take seriously, and Swift pointed the way for me.

Swift helped turn my contempt for the foolishness I saw in

others into compassion. While contempt leads to the cage of isolation, compassion leads to a freedom found only in community. For despite being charged by his critics as a misanthrope, Swift demonstrates that actually only one whose expectations are high can be as disappointed (and amused) at human behavior as he was. In an age that would bring about the rise of the individual captured so well in *Jane Eyre,* Swift valued community and friendship.

But even more significantly, Swift helped me to realize my own foolishness. It was so easy to see it in others, much harder to recognize it in myself. "Satire is a sort of glass," Swift said, "wherein beholders do generally discover everybody's face but their own; which is the chief reason for that kind reception it meets with in the world, and that so very few are offended with it." I had long loved satire, but with these words, one of the greatest satirists who ever lived was satirizing me. Did I love satire only because in it I saw everyone else but me? Was I as blind to my own faults as Swift showed others to be? It seemed so.

My tailor-made-for-me version of sexual morality worked temporarily, but its rationalized approach had itself a couple of deep flaws. One—if I planned to have sex with anyone but myself (and, yes, that was the plan), then how could I be sure that the other person's individual sexual morality would fit mine? Of course, I could ask. But if we were all in the business of making up our own sexual morality, what was to prevent the person in question from making up a new one when it suited him? Two—the real problem (although I couldn't quite see it then), was that having made up my sexual morality, I really had no grounds for dismissing that of anyone else which happened to be different from mine. Without a context of community standards—religious or otherwise—we were all just individuals with warring symbols for this thing called sex.

Both knowledge and honesty are essential to true freedom, even (or especially) sexual freedom. I certainly do not wish for a return to the kind of Pollyanna approach to sex so characteristic of previous generations; I harbor no desire to return to the tragic ignorance of my mother's youth or that of Tess in *Tess of the D'Urbervilles.* Yet at the same time, none of the scenes I described above, common versions of sexual freedom the world offers, reflect true freedom. They symbolize sexual freedom, but disconnected as they are from the real purpose and meaning of sex, they are false symbols. Imagine two substances that look the same, say, white flour and rat poison. Imagine the symbol for each, a cluster of wheat and a skull and cross bones, placed on the wrong package. This is what happens when a symbol is separated from the reality it is supposed to reflect. It signifies the wrong thing. And it can lead to death rather than life, to a cage rather than freedom.

While I saw fit to devise an individual moral code suited to me, Swift recognized that real wisdom comes not from the voice within, but from the collective wisdom of the community of humankind over the ages. Yes, from God ultimately, but in our imperfect human understanding and application, strength of heart and mind—wisdom—is built in community, not individually. In judging the vice and folly of individuals, Swift used the scales of collective wisdom. And since the purpose of satire is to correct human folly and wickedness, it seems that Swift both sought and expected improvements, the very definition of optimism, not the pessimism with which some of his critics charge him because of his biting satire. Swift's frankness, his realism, his high view of God and humanity, and his belief in the essential nature of community all shed light on one of the funniest and most poignant spins he puts on sex in *Gulliver's Travels,* a point he slips in so subtly it's easy to miss. But once recognized, it is powerful.

For Swift, symbol is always reflective of reality. Thus when he offers a crude sexual depiction, it is not for mere exploitation. Swift's concern was never the merely physical (this was an obsession for which he faulted many of his contemporaries in his scientific age), but for the human, which includes both the physical and spiritual aspects of our being.

The Lilliputians who are small in stature turn out to be just as small in terms of their minds and hearts. Conversely, the giant people of Brobdingnag are some of the biggest-hearted citizens Gulliver encounters. When the maids of honor in Voyage Two make tiny Gulliver into a sort of toy, Swift demonstrates that in doing so, the women are denying, and thus degrading, Gulliver's manhood and, therefore, his essential humanity, too. When the fe-male Yahoo in Voyage Four tries to attack Gulliver sexually (prov-ing they are of the same species), Gulliver's revulsion points to his self-hatred as well as his delusions about his own humanity; what Gulliver despises about the Yahoos are the ugly and animal as-pects of the human condition, aspects that, as Swift shows, we must accept in order to embrace our full humanity.

Sex, for Swift, is never separated from our humanity. His coarse, humorous depictions of the efforts we make to force such a separation are designed to expose the folly and destruction of any such attempt. But sometimes readers simply take offense, thereby missing the important lessons altogether. It seems that many who have been taught to express offense at such frankness about human sexuality and human nature probably behave in a more Swiftian fashion in private and among friends. This is yet one more example of the compartmentalizing we do so easily and thoughtlessly in modern life, which Swift foresaw in the early mod-ern age in which he lived.

The very thing Swift was warning against—the attempt to sep-arate the physical nature of our humanity from our spiritual na-ture—was epitomized in one of my psychology classes in college one day when the professor announced that we would be viewing in class an educational film on sex. "The film is graphic," he droned from the front of the classroom as he turned out the lights. I imagined it to be some R-rated, artsy sort of graphic images or the sort of smutty *Go Ask Alice* or *Fear of Flying* scenes I'd been reading in books since I was twelve. But apparently my imagina-tion was too small. The course was called Psychology of Love and Sex, but it turned out to be a whole lot about sex and not so much about love. The professor was a sex therapist in his day job—go figure. The class wasn't all bad, though. It was an interesting and helpful elective well-suited to my major in Social work. Plus, he graded on a curve, so that meant I was getting all A's. Despite the professor's warning, then, I settled back into my seat near the rear of the room. But his warning was not enough. What ap-peared, larger-than-life, on the screen at the front of the room was not very arty. In fact, I was pretty sure it was straight-up porn.

Oh, sure, the film was presented in the guise of a documentary with strategically-placed cameras providing close-up, REALLY CLOSE-UP, shots of numerous bodies and body parts engaged in various sexual acts, with the terms for those acts in both their clinical and slang forms, dubbed in. Where exactly did they put those cameras? I had no idea what the educational value of this exercise was supposed to be. I suspected that the professor was doing some sort of experiment on us, the students, given that he'd taken an anonymous survey of our sex lives at the start of the semester and then announced the results, including this tidbit: "according to the survey, one person in this class is a virgin"—as if that wasn't supposed to make every student in the class look around and try to figure out which one of us was a virgin or a liar. I gave the film five minutes, then I walked out feeling angry and violated. When I returned to the next class, I acted as though nothing had happened although inside I was still seething. But I'd be damned if he didn't give me the "A" I knew I was earning, so I played it cool. At the end of the semester, I got my "A."

This very separation of the physical from the spiritual was chief among Swift's concerns. And perhaps this separation is no more consequential in any area of human experience than sex. My own double-mindedness in embracing an individualistic sexual ethic on the one hand, and taking offense at the dancers in cages at the heavy metal concert and the film shown in my psychology class on the other, was precisely the folly Swift satirized almost three centuries earlier. My Psychology professor made the same error—separating the physical from the spiritual—with the film he showed. The film depicted sex in a purely clinical, scientific fashion: images unadorned by any narrative or context, isolated from any emotional, relational, or moral context, accompanied merely by various terms, as though human sexuality could possibly be reduced to this.

Of course, there are errors that go in the other direction—denial of the physical aspect of human nature and human sexuality in favor of a lofty and impossible kind of idealism that exists outside of the world of physical embodiment. Swift had something to say about this kind of mistake, too. Such idealism, or romanticism, in fact, was a frequent target of Swift's satire.

His most brutal skewering of the human tendency to romanticize love to the point of losing grip with reality is in his poem, "The Lady's Dressing Room." Here Swift describes a young man sneaking into the vacated dressing room of his beloved where he experiences, upon discovering the tools of her beauty secrets and her dirtied toiletries, quite a rude awakening (to put it mildly). The rudest discovery of all is what he finds within a deceptively-decorous box. At seeing this, the poet tells us, Strephon falls "into fits" to learn that his beloved "Celia, Celia, Celia shits!" Swift bitingly points out the folly of so elevating our romantic partners that we forget the reality they are human, too. This is one (certainly not the only) error reflected in pornographic works like those pornographic magazines Farrah Hair and I studied that day so long ago. There is nothing "real" about the de-contextualized and de-spiritualized portrayals of sex depicted on those pages: the symbols are disconnected from the substance.

Yet, Swift is an equal-opportunity offender. In another work, he points out the error made at the opposite extreme by poking fun at those who aspire to a love that is only spiritual and not physical:

> Lovers for the sake of celestial converse are but another sort of Platonics, who pretend to see stars and heaven in ladies' eyes, and to look or think no lower; but the same pit is provided for both; and they seem a perfect moral to the story of that philosopher, who, while his thoughts and eyes were fixed upon the constellations, found himself seduced by his lower parts into a ditch.

By denying human nature—which is both physical and spiritual—Swift's illustration proves, we are bound to end up in the gutter. The air in a balloon squeezed on one end will burst out the other end eventually. It's the nature of reality. Perhaps that's why the Victorian age, which was known for its prudishness on the one hand, had a thriving underground trade in prostitution.

One of Swift's profound lessons in *Gulliver's Travels* on the holism of human sexuality—that it is both physical and spiritual—begins with one of his characteristic naughty-isms: easy to miss but impossible to ignore once captured. In the first chapter, Gulliver relates that being unable to afford continuing his studies at Cambridge, he is apprenticed to a surgeon, Mr. James Bates. For the next several paragraphs, he mentions this Mr. Bates, his master, the good Mr. Bates, his good master several times. The last time he describes him as his "good Master Bates." The pun is intended. It seems puerile and silly when it appears as it does so early on in the book, in isolation, but when we connect it to an important part in the end of *Gulliver's Travels,* this seemingly insignificant, naughty, little pun becomes downright profound.

In each of Gulliver's voyages to strange lands, he has encountered strange inhabitants and strange ways and reported his encounters with his characteristic naiveté. But in his last voyage to the country of the Houyhnhnms (the horse people), he returns to his native England changed like never before: he comes back as a misanthrope, a hater of the human race. He is repelled by humankind. He tries with great difficulty to overcome his repugnance. The most telling instance of what really amounts to Gulliver's pride is his confession that,

> At the time I am writing, it is five years since my last return to England. During the first year, I could not endure my wife or children in my presence; the very smell of them was intolerable; much less could I suffer them to eat in the same room. To this hour they dare not presume to touch my bread, or drink out of the same cup, neither was I ever able to let one of them take me by the hand.

This is the most damning information Swift the author could provide about Gulliver the character. For Swift, you recall, is an Anglican clergyman. When he describes Gulliver as refusing to allow his family, his wife even, to touch his "bread" or "drink out of the same cup," what Swift is describing is Gulliver's willing exclusion of his family, even his wife, from nothing less than communion. The truth is easy to miss in *Gulliver's Travels* because it's easy to miss in life, too, since we underestimate the significance of symbols. In so doing, we miss the substance the symbol points us toward.

Consider the blood sacrifices made in ancient cultures. Such systems of religious and cultural belief are far beyond my ability to explain rationally. But I do understand something of the way such acts connect symbol and reality: blood sacrifices are literally matters of life and death, and at the same time, they symbolize that the things they are sacrificed for—whether sin, fertility, obedience to God, worship of a deity—are, literally, matters of life and death. In such systems, symbol and reality are inseparable in a way that is foreign to the modern mindset.

Consider the act of communion as it is undertaken by Christians. There is nothing magical about partaking of the elements, be they bread and wine or their tamer, modern counterparts, juice and crackers. But the acts of chewing the substance that symbolizes Christ's body and drinking the dark liquid that symbolizes Christ's blood reflects the essential relationship between symbol and substance. (Even the different understandings among Catholic and Protestant Christians of what does and doesn't happen in communion in partaking the elements is less important than our agreement about the significance of the act to Christian worship.) The spiritual and religious symbolism of communion is embodied in the physical acts of seeing, touching, smelling, hearing, and tasting.

The genius of Swift is in distinguishing the false symbol from the true, and in reminding us that the power of a symbol arises from a community—not an individual—that agrees upon its meaning. Thus *Gulliver's Travels* ends where it begins, with imagery of isolation and the lack of sexual connection with another human being that reveal the errors of modern individualism.

As bizarre and as diverse as are all of the adventures Gulliver undergoes and the places he visits, the consistent element in each of these is Gulliver's skewed individual perspective. You see, Gulliver's "gullibility," his naiveté, is rooted in the fact that he judges most everything according to his own particular vantage point, regardless of any larger context, failing to consider the view of the community he is in. So when Gulliver describes the land in Lilliput as smooth and flat, he neglects to consider that it is his immense size that renders it so; to the Lilliputians, the land is as varied as it would be to Gulliver in England. The incident described above in which Gulliver tries to convince his reader that he has not had a sexual liaison with the Lilliputian lady demonstrates that his perspective is so distorted that he doesn't even recognize the physical impossibility of such an event. By the time he reaches the final voyage to the country of the gentle and peaceable horses, Gulliver loses entirely his perspective of what it means to be human. So when he returns to his home country, to his wife and family, his perspective is distorted to the point that he rejects the human community—and with this he becomes isolated in his cage of self, preferring, he tells us, the company of the horses.

Perspective is one of the central themes in *Gulliver's Travels*, more specifically, the unreliability of human perspective in isolation. Reliable perspective comes not from merely an individual vantage point, but from a view that is both high and broad, one that considers the view from eternity and the view from history, the view of Providence and the view of the community. Gulliver's essential failure, from the start of his travels to their end, is his failure to recognize the fallibility of his own perspective.

In learning who I was as an individual, I needed to remember the community I came from. After all, I had wound my way along the serpentine path toward becoming my self through the guidance of that community: a father and mother who taught me about God, a mother who read books to me and told me how I was different from others, a brother who believed in me, and the community of people I came from who were fiercely independent, who talked a little funny, and whose faces bore the lines of the rugged land. I carried my family's history within me, the name of my grandmother, the lessons of my mother, and the affirmation of my father. I needed more than my own perspective, although, like Gulliver, I didn't quite see that.

I was given a new perspective at Memorial Auditorium, at a kitschy heavy metal concert of all places. My seat way up high with a godlike vantage point offered a view of those women in cages of their own choosing and of me in the cage of my choosing.

8

Know Thyself: *Death of a Salesman*

A man is ever apt to contemplate himself out
of all proportion to his surroundings.

—Christina Rossetti

I was finally here.

I had been anticipating college since the first time I heard
about it. I think that was when I was about seven and my family
hosted some young women from a travelling singing group visit-
ing our church. The young women were college students, and I
was fascinated by them. Not by what they were doing in their
choir—travelling around from church to church, singing and what-
not—but by the idea of being a college student. I wasn't even sure
what college was, exactly, but it enchanted me. Neither of my parents had gone to college, but my dad's two younger siblings had
gone to college, including Uncle Bobby who had lived in our basement and was the coolest old person I knew.

Here I was. Everything was fresh and strange—but also,
somehow, just as I had always expected it to be. It never crossed
my mind that I would go on to become a professor and never,
ever leave college once I'd begun. All I knew at this point was that
if school had been a crush, college was a full-blown affair.

The excitement helped lessen, if only a little, the pain of my
breakup with Randy. The drama had taken place just a couple of
weeks before the start of school, amidst the chaos of my parents
moving out-of-state. My father had the chance to take an early re-
tirement from the international corporation where he'd worked
for 25 years, and I moved in with my Uncle Bobby at the last
minute. I could stick to my college plans, and I didn't have to be
separated from Randy. I'm not sure how many more dramatic life

changes might possibly have been crammed into those few weeks in the life of an eighteen-year-old. I'm sure plenty have gone through a great deal more, but I hadn't. And plenty more have gone through a painful breakup, too, but I hadn't done that either.

Besides, no one's breakup is as bad as your own.

Randy had been growing steadily distant over the summer, although he kept insisting nothing was wrong, and I chose to believe him. Perhaps I was too distracted by all the other changes going on. One night, the last night I was supposed to spend at my parents' house, now nearly empty except for boxes and a few large pieces of furniture, Randy called from work to cancel our plans because he would have to work late. Something told me this was problematic. After a while, I drove to the steakhouse where he had started as a bus boy. I wasn't sure why I headed there at one in the morning or what I expected to find, but I know I didn't expect to find him sitting in his car in the parking lot with the assistant manager. I'd met this assistant manager before and knew she was a few years older than us, recently divorced, rather pretty, and extremely, well, outgoing. I'm not sure what they were doing before I pulled up next to them in his car, but he certainly wasn't working as he told me he would be.

It was the moment of crisis—not quite the one I thought it was at the time, but one I see clearly now. All of my life up to this point had been a tug-of-war within myself between two competing forces: acceptance by others and acceptance of myself.

That night, I won.

I stayed long enough to hear him offer a tepid excuse and a slightly more passionate appeal for me not to leave. But I left. While I may have been a fool for him, I wasn't an idiot. I got back into my car and left the two of them in the otherwise deserted parking lot and headed to my last night at home.

I'd never been on this road at this time of night. At around two a.m., not a person or vehicle was in sight. I'd never seen the city look so empty. I drove down the middle of a six-lane swath of silent discount stores and fast food joints rising up from a bog of empty parking lots. Everything seemed to move in slow motion. A canopy of hazy yellow light arced overhead, enveloping me in an orb of silence. It was like being inside a snow globe: my world had been shaken, but instead of glittery snow, a sickly yellow fluorescent glow fell down around me, suffocating and choking me.

Suddenly, the eerie yellow light flashed red. I'd been driving slowly, too slowly, my eyesight dimmed by tears, and weaving suspiciously, too. The officer asked how much I'd been drinking and I told him nothing. He looked at me incredulously, and I blubbered out the whole story. He let me go with a warning.

Still in a daze, I started college just a few days later. I had looked forward to this moment for most of my life—this was not at all what I had hoped it would be like. But I had been dreaming about going to college a lot longer than I'd been with Randy, I reminded myself, so I tried to focus on the things I had anticipated for years: the comforting weight of thick books, the rainbow colors of highlighters and pens for marking textbooks that belonged to me (unlike the loaners given out in high school), the crack of a tight textbook spine when I opened it the first time, the crispness of the college-ruled paper I'd use to take notes, and especially the literature anthology that seemed to me to be a sacred text with its tissue thin pages and tiny print in double columns. I was looking forward most to my English class.

Randy had been very possessive, so I was eager to make up for lost time. I made friends with anyone and everyone. By the end of my first semester, I was seeing three guys: a banker, an Ivy League frat boy, and a guitarist in a band. I gloried in the absence of the cliques that so shaped life in junior high and high school. Here people of various ages and backgrounds met simply one on one rather than within the context of a clique, club, or an artificial grouping based on year of birth.

For the first time in my life, I was on my own, really on my own: no parents, no boyfriend, no best friend to influence my choices. So I imagined, more freely than ever before, what I really wanted for my life. Of all the subjects I took and loved in college, the subject of myself turned out to be the most important one. But when I speak of the subject of myself, I do not mean the sort of navel-gazing that turns the eyes of the soul inward. Rather I mean the study of myself in my rightful place within the vast universe, the same universe that opened up before me among the array of far worthier subjects I encountered in college. High school was too full of easy work and easy distractions, but in college I learned to take wonder in the world around me. In focusing my attention on things much bigger than myself, ironically, I learned who I was. It's the lesson, once again, that beholding is becoming.

As far back as the ancient Greeks, wisdom has dictated, "Know thyself." But this is not so easy. Which is probably why so many stories, old and new, center on this quest.

A popular movie from a few years ago stars Julia Roberts as a woman named Maggie who repeatedly gets cold feet and ditches a succession of grooms at the altar. A reporter (played by Richard Gere) hears about the infamous "runaway bride" (the title of the movie) and publishes a story about her. When he gets a number of facts wrong, he has to follow up with a more detailed investigation. In interviewing the men this woman, Maggie, has left behind, the reporter (who, predictably—spoiler alert—ends up with the bride by the end of the movie), accidentally stumbles upon an interesting and telling tidbit about Maggie: all the men Maggie has jilted tell him that Maggie likes her eggs prepared exactly the way each of them likes their eggs. The problem is each of these men likes his eggs a different way. Upon further investigation, the reporter finds that in each of her relationships, Maggie has taken on not only the man's taste in eggs, but his interests, hobbies, lifestyle and his very identity as her own—leaving, of course, no identity of her own. In each relationship, rather than being herself, Maggie becomes merely a female version of each of these very different men. She doesn't do this knowingly, of course, but nevertheless there it is: the runaway bride hasn't been running from these men all this time—she's been running away from herself.

In many areas of life, self-knowledge is crucially important to making wise choices, the sort of choices that lead to a fulfilling life. For what would be the wise choice for you, might not be the wise choice for your neighbor. Of course, in making choices between right and wrong, right is always the wise choice, but many, if not most, of our daily choices deal not with right or wrong, but with shades of right. Probably the most significant area in which this is true is in our choice of daily work, and it is in the area of work that Willy in Arthur Miller's 1949 *Death of a Salesman* experiences the tragic consequences of failing to know who he is.

Another spoiler alert: the salesman dies. But what makes this death tragic—in the classical sense—is that death could have been avoided. Arthur Miller purposely emulated the classical tragedy model in writing his modern tragedy of the "common man." In this case, the fatal error of the tragic hero, the salesman Willy Loman, is combined with the force of fate manifest in the social context of the hyper-capitalist, consumer culture of mid-1950s America. As in classical tragedy, all is not entirely lost, for illumination is gained, arguably, for Willy, and even more clearly for his son, Biff.

This social context that Willy finds himself in—the consumer-driven, appearance-obsessed culture of modern America, takes the place fate holds in ancient tragedies. However, in the classical model, the tragic end is not brought about by fate alone, but in combination with the tragic hero's actions, actions rooted in some tragic flaw. For many a tragic hero, that tragic flaw is pride. Willy's pride is revealed in various ways in his downward spiral. Willy is too proud to ask his grown sons for financial help when he desperately needs it (though they are pretty much worthless anyway), and too proud to resist buying for his wife and home things he can't afford, and too proud to be honest with his wife—or even to be honest with himself—about his failings. This lack of honesty with himself is what gets us closer to the real tragic flaw in this tragic hero: Willy's failure to know himself.

One of the first people I met in college was Dee Dee, who was in my Psych 101 class. Dee Dee was a yahoo. She was from the south side, one of the roughest parts of the city. One Friday, I went home with Dee Dee to spend the night at her house. She lived in an old rambling Victorian, but not the kind that had been renovated by yuppies. This one had peeling paint on the outside and scarred wooden floors and wallpaper grayed by cigarette smoke on the inside. Dee Dee's mother and uncounted siblings lived here. We left the house at an hour when most people were going to bed and crawled around the streets of her neighborhood all night, making stops at the corner bars. I'd lived in two states and half a dozen towns in my eighteen years of life. That so many people's ancestral roots were planted in a single neighborhood for generations was strange to me. I was fascinated, but I felt far from home. At some point, in the wee hours, I lost track of Dee Dee and had to be directed to her home by someone in one of the ubiquitous corner bars, which didn't close until five a.m. It wasn't until about that time when I crept back into Dee Dee's house and found an unoccupied bed that had blankets but no sheets and crawled in to sleep as best I could. Dee Dee didn't show up for class that Monday, and she missed a lot more classes after that. She didn't return to school the next semester. I never even tried to contact her.

Joyce, who was in my Philosophy class, had transferred from another school where she'd been a sorority sister. She hinted about needing to change schools after some kind of sexual assault involving a sorority event, but I didn't pry further. Joyce lived with her divorced mother in an elegant apartment in North Buffalo and played piano. We went out one night to an upscale dance club and she drank coffee liqueurs—which seemed to me a bit like drinking dessert all night, a bit too quaint for a rum-and-Coke girl like me. Why Joyce wanted to be friends with me was a mystery. Where I was Cyndi Lauper rock-chick-ish, she was polo-shirt preppy girl-ish. I wore stone-washed jeans, and she wore pearls. She cut her dark hair in a classic bob, and my hair always ran wild. I realized that she must have had even less a sense of herself than I had ever had, and seeing that helped me to see myself even more clearly. Maybe she had just developed an avoidance reflex to the sorority type because of her bad experience at her other school. I don't know. She persisted in trying to make plans with me, and I consented a few times, but did my best to nudge on a natural parting of the ways.

Somewhere between these two extremes—the skanky party girl and the prissy sorority drop out—was there a good friend for me? I hadn't made many new friends when I'd moved to this city a year and a half prior and left my best friend Rachael behind, because I had hooked up with Randy so quickly and had stupidly centered my whole life on him. How could I ever find real friends until I knew who I was?

I had spent eighteen years trying to become myself, but I was just now learning who it was that I was becoming. And who I was becoming was not necessarily the person I had in mind. Perhaps that person was born the night I drove away from that restaurant parking lot and refused to be either a doormat or a fool.

I had declared my major as social work when I applied to college. I had even made my final choice for college based on its social work program. I had decided to pursue this field because of my interest in psychiatry which I had discovered, naturally, by reading a book, *Sybil*, about a woman with multiple personality disorder. Many years later, the whole story—which, like *Go Ask Alice,* was supposed to be true—was exposed as a sham. But I had read lots of similar books and as a result thought I wanted to help people.

But a funny thing happened. I discovered the study of English literature. Of course, I had known about English before. I'd been reading my entire life. In school, English was one of those subjects required of every student every year. I had always loved it and done well in it. But besides Mrs. Lovejoy, I had never met anyone who took English seriously. Most of my high school English teachers were either tired or hankering to go back to Woodstock or both. I don't think I even knew until I got to college that you could actually major in English. That sounded to me, at first, like catching frogs: something you do for fun but not something you work at seriously.

On my first day of freshman composition that first semester of college, the professor gave us an in-class writing assignment: describe your life ten years from now. That would be easy.

But as I started to write, I realized it was going to be hard.

As I've already said, I was planning to be a social worker. I'd planned to marry Randy, too. That wasn't going to happen. Everything seemed upside down. I thought about the snow globe again, and how shaken my world was. I looked at my left hand holding one of my new pens and noticed the nakedness of my ring finger where I had, until just days ago, worn a promise ring: a blue stone wrapped by a gold band that formed, romantically, into the shape of a heart on either side of the stone. I looked up from my hand and stared out the window at the leaves, deceptively green on this late August day, as they shimmied in the breeze. A big piece of my vision for my life ten years from now was hazy. But, slowly, other parts came into focus. I sat and stared at the fading summer outside the classroom window and finally wrote. I kept writing until the class was over, and the professor collected the essays. For both of these things—the uncertainty at first, and the clarity that grew as I wrote—I remember this essay vividly.

Because of that writing assignment, I had a new plan.

Looking back, I count it as a kind of divine grace that I entered college with no boyfriend in tow. I was free to get to know myself by beholding the larger world unfurling around me in all its wonder.

It is exactly this knowledge of self that the runaway bride—who doesn't even know what kind of eggs she likes—lacks. I can see that it's the kind of knowledge I lacked, too, in losing myself in the object of my first love. I can see this lack in the real world all around me. I see it in the marriage breakups between people who come to see themselves differently than they once did. How much of this "difference" is owing to change (which certainly does occur as the self in an evolving entity of sorts) and how much of it to simply knowing oneself better? Similarly, a friend of mine has struggled with an eating disorder since she was a pre-teen. When she finally embarked on the long, winding road to recovery in her twenties, she found herself in a veritable state of adolescence. Having denied herself so much of what life offers for so long, she had to set out to discover many of her likes and dislikes for the very first time—from what flavor of ice cream she liked, to what kind of man she was attracted to, to what kind of work she wanted to do. Denying oneself the pleasures of food is just the most obvious symptom of a greater problem of denying oneself the pleasures of life in general. That is a lot to catch up on when most people of that age are getting settled into marriage, career, and raising a family.

Knowing oneself has tremendous importance for all of the major life decisions one might make. Making life choices that are in line with who one is—who one was created to be—leads to a more fulfilling life. I know that "self-fulfillment" has become a dirty word for those who rightly understand that life is not "all about me," but about a greater purpose. This is true. At the same time, each of us is created as a unique individual with unique gifts, talents, and callings that were designed for a purpose. Self-fulfillment doesn't necessarily mean selfish fulfillment. It can mean fulfillment of all that one was created to be. The satisfaction one feels at having achieved one's rightful desires is no more selfish or wrong a thing than the satisfaction of the apple tree in bringing forth the fruit it was designed to bear.

But sometimes we mistake other people's desires as our own. It is easy to confuse our love or admiration for another person with a desire for the things that person loves or admires. But just because we like another person, we don't necessarily have to like the things that person likes. What makes one person happy isn't going to make the next person happy. A student I once had told her friends that someday she wanted to live in an old farmhouse with lots of dogs, just like I do. The trouble is that she didn't seem to even like dogs, let alone farm animals. She was mistaking her fondness for me for a fondness for the things I love. Such trans-ferences of affection can occur, to be sure—as my love for the things Mrs. Lovejoy loved shows. But the love of a person must be distinguished from a love of those things loved by the person we love, just as we learn to distinguish ourselves from others.

In college, I discovered more in this world to love than I had ever known before. I loved studying and writing papers. I loved class discussions. I loved English. I did not love social work or its required classes like statistics. I hated statistics so much that I had to take the slow class, held over two semesters rather than one. But I loved English. These were the things pointing me toward my true vocation. Thomas Merton says, "Discovering vocation does not mean scrambling toward some prize just beyond my reach but accepting the treasure of true self I already possess. Vo-cation does not come from a voice out there calling me to be something I am not. It comes from a voice in here calling me to be the person I was born to be, to fulfill the original selfhood given me at birth by God." In college, I was discovering that treasure of true self I already possessed. I was discovering my calling.

Willy Loman, on the other hand, never heeded his calling. He never fulfilled his true vocation. For, he was never meant to be a salesman. And that is the heart of the tragedy.

When the play opens, Willy is old. His memory is failing. He is weary. But his profession, sales, by its very nature, is based on the new and improved, not the old and outdated. Interestingly, the play never reveals what it is that Willy and his company sell. In the modern age of the disinterested middleman (such as Willy), this doesn't matter: sales is sales. And sales—regardless of the product being sold—are driven by appearance, and Willy's appearances are failing in every respect. Willy constantly tells his sons that the key to success in life is being "well-liked." But as his appearances decline and his old contacts disappear, Willy's sales, naturally, diminish. As Willy feels more and more like a failure, these feelings put into motion a self-fulfilling prophecy, and his failures increase until he is fired and his world crashes.

The title of the work has two references in the play, and they are inextricably linked: the first is the ending, already discussed, which leaves the salesman Willy Loman dead; the other reference is found in passing in the play, in a story Willy tells his boss just before his boss fires him. That story is of another salesman, Dave Singleman whom Willy met years before when Dave was 84 years old. Dave, Willy says, would "put on his green velvet slippers … and pick up his phone and call the buyers, and without ever leaving his room, he made his living." At that moment, seeing Dave's success, Willy decided that "selling was the greatest career a man could want." "What could be more satisfying?" he asks. And when Dave Singleman died all those years ago, Willy tells his boss, he "died the death of a salesman. In his green velvet slippers in the smoker of the New York, New Haven, and Hartford, going into Boston – when he died, hundreds of salesmen and buyers were at his funeral." At this turning point in his life, long before the play opens, Willy abandoned the plans he had made to follow his father to Alaska in pursuit of an "adventurous" and "self-reliant" life and instead turned to a career in sales. This is his tragic error.

Willy has mistaken the means of success for one person as the means for himself. He even has a mistaken notion of success itself. In fact, *Death of a Salesman* is as much about the true meaning of success, more specifically, the American Dream, as it is about the death of Willy Loman.

After Willy's death, immediately following his funeral, Willy's son Biff recognizes his father's fatal error and says of Willy, in the play's Requiem, "He had the wrong dreams. All, all wrong," Biff tells his mother and their neighbor Charley as they look at Willy's grave. "He never knew who he was," Biff continues. "The man didn't know who he was."

And Biff is right, as ample evidence in the play shows. In adopting Dave Singleman's dream as his own, Willy makes the very error that *Jane Eyre* is tempted to make: he follows someone else's dream instead of his own. Willy makes the mistake of seeing the means of someone else's happiness and success as a means for his own happiness and success. But, the ingredients for success—skills, drive, circumstances and, yes, a certain amount of luck—aren't the same from person to person. It is a grave mistake to look at someone else's source of satisfaction and see it as the means to one's own. But this is exactly what Willy does in observing the success of Dave Singleman in being a salesman and believing it could be the means of his own success. The results of Willy's mistake are far from successful, for in assuming that someone else's dream could serve as his own, Willy's true failure is in failing to know himself.

In his book, *God at Work,* Gene Edward Veith discusses the idea of vocation and, in particular, the working out of that view in the Protestant tradition, beginning with Martin Luther's teachings on the subject. As Veith points out, it is significant that God created both man and woman to work and called them to do so before the fall. It is part of God's original design to work, not because our work saves us, but because work meets the needs of our neighbors. Through our work, we serve others.

Not only did God design mankind in a general way to work,

but he also designed and equipped individuals toward specific kinds of work. Veith writes, "Even your wants—your desires, your dreams, your choices—are a function of who you are ... The doctrine of vocation has to do with the mystery of individuality, how God creates each human being to be different from all the rest and gives each a unique calling in every stage of life." God calls people to fulfill the roles for which he has designed them. In other words, according to Veith, "Our vocation is not something we choose for ourselves. It is something to which we are called."

As I am writing this—in bed with my laptop on a late evening—one of my three dogs approaches, wanting to climb up and snuggle with me. She's a German Shorthaired Pointer, a bird dog. But she's never been hunting. In fact, when my husband target practices or sights in his gun, she jumps into the bathtub to hide in the darkness behind the shower curtain. Yet she cannot entirely escape her breeding. This breed of dog was developed primarily to point birds for the hunter and then retrieve the birds once they have been brought down. Generations of cultivation of certain qualities, of instincts, cannot be denied. Lucy may not hunt, but she will point squirrels all day long and pick up and carry with a soft mouth any shoe left lying on the floor—she will bring it to you as with as much pride as if she were retrieving a delicate quail from a dense thicket on the edge of a wood. Seeing her gently and proudly carry a shoe or slipper in her mouth—she never chews, only gently holds, just as she would correctly do with a bird—makes me think even more about our calling, about the things we were created to do, and how it is so difficult to escape that, though many of us do, whether out of ignorance, necessity, tragedy, or fear.

In a way, the classical view of tragedy (as we saw in *Tess of the D'Urbervilles*) parallels a Christian understanding, for in tragedy there is always an outside force—whether it is understood as fate, prophecy, or the intervention of the gods—that plays a part in the outcome of events for the hero. In a similar way, vocation is "out of our control," Veith says. It is, at least in part, "a function of the particular gifts God has given us, but we cannot know our vocation purely by looking inside ourselves." By beholding the world around us, our rightful place in the world is revealed. We can't simply decide apart from an understanding of the world we find ourselves in that we want to be a brain surgeon or a concert pianist and then do it. A number of factors in the areas of both nature (our inborn abilities) and nurture (our upbringing and opportunities) must be present in order to pursue a vocation successfully. This is why it is so essential for one to "know thyself," so as to set out on a path that will be successful in the most important sense of that word. One must know not only one's particular gifts and talents, but one's passions, too, for all of these contribute to success.

It's hard to tell real passion from passing fancy, though. Like most children, I had many interests. But from the get-go, I ruled out two professions: teaching and nursing. I'm not sure why, exactly. Probably simply because they seemed too typical for girls, and the rebel in me resisted.

It's hard to find the best way to fulfill a passion, too. In my preteen and early teen years, I wanted to be a veterinarian and even set up a sort of informal internship with my horse vet when I was in Junior High. But a love for animals—even a lifelong love as mine has turned out to be—does not automatically translate into a love of cutting and stitching and medicating animals—or the kind of studies required beforehand. Then I read *Sybil* and became fascinated with multiple personalities and victims of child abuse. I decided I wanted to become a psychiatrist. This goal stuck for a few years, but by the time I was heading off to college, my earlier love of school had fizzled out from lackluster classes and bleary-eyed teachers. My academic ambitions likewise were watered down to the more practical goal of becoming a social worker. The degrees required for becoming a psychiatrist would require at least five years of study; those for a social worker would require no more than five.

Clearly, I had yet to know myself. For one thing, I ended up spending more than eight years on my Ph.D. Even more importantly—and it wasn't until years after I had abandoned the goal of becoming a social worker that I came to understand this—I am a person rather lacking in some of the most essential qualities for such a calling: namely, certain forms of kindness, compassion, patience, and at least a reasonable tolerance for government red tape. Fortunately, even before I knew myself well enough to see these shortcomings, I had discovered that literature was not only an enjoyable pastime but also, *lo and behold!* a legitimate academic pursuit. It took several more years for me to discover (quite serendipitously) that teaching was what I was created to do. But that's another story.

Death of a Salesman provides hints about who Willy really is, though he doesn't see it himself. The play begins as Willy's life—and his dream of success—are rapidly unraveling. As his life begins to deteriorate, so does Willy's mind. He can no longer distinguish between reality and illusion. These are the fitting consequences of living an entire life based on the delusion of a false dream. And why did Willy's life as a salesman constitute the pursuit of a false dream? Because, as the play makes clear, Willy suppressed his real nature and sold himself out to become something he wasn't called to be. As we learn from various revelations in the play, it wasn't making sales that made Willy happy; it was making things with his hands. Reflecting upon Willy's self-inflicted death, his son Biff remarks,

"There were a lot of nice days. When he'd come home from a trip; or on Sundays, making the stoop; finishing the cellar; putting on the new porch; when he built the bedroom; and put up the garage. You know something, Charley, there's more of him in that front stoop than in all the sales he made."

To which Charley responds, "Yeah. He was a happy man with a batch of cement." Other clues point to Willy's calling as an outdoorsman who works with his hands: in one of his frequent reveries he tells his older brother Ben that he moved to Brooklyn—before it was built up—because it had "snakes and rabbits." Later Willy complains to his wife Linda about the closing in of their neighborhood: "The grass don't grow anymore, you can't raise a carrot in the backyard. They should've had a law against apartment houses. Remember those two beautiful elm trees out there? When I and Biff hung the swing between them?" Working with his hands was even part of his natural inheritance, for we learn that Willy's father, "a very great and wild-hearted man," was a salesman, but the products he sold, flutes, were those he made with his own hands—and played, too.

But Willy's error is twice over. For not only does he reject his true calling, he derides the outdoorsy, manual work he was called to do. When he overhears his son Biff lament the family's urban life, saying, "We should be mixing cement on some open plain, or—or carpenters. A carpenter is allowed to whistle!" Willy responds scoffingly, "Your grandfather was better than a carpenter." Indeed the deep rift between Willy and his elder son is rooted in Willy's insistence on false values, values that betray his rightful inheritance and his true self. These false values that have become the vortex by which Willy's life is spiraling out of control are captured by the whipped American cheese that Linda offers Willy in Act 1 when he returns home, tired and defeated, from an unsuccessful sales trip. In a rare moment of authenticity, Willy, who likes Swiss cheese—an aged, real cheese, not a simulation—wonders aloud, "How can they whip cheese?" Despite his surface-level adherence to the materialistic values of the modern middle class, Willy's soul recoils at everything represented in a cheese product twice removed from the real thing.

Caught between these two opposing forces—the false consumer values Willy has raised his sons with and the pull of the traditional values of the preceding generation—both of Willy's sons embody the results of these mixed messages, each in his own way. Happy, as his name implies, is in blissful denial about his father's failures—and his own. Biff, meanwhile, teeters precariously between rejecting his father in pursuit of his authentic identity on one hand, and trying to fulfill the natural desire for a father's unconditional love and acceptance on the other. In two poignant scenes toward the play's end when events are spiraling toward their tragic outcome, both Biff and Willy seem to gain illumination into this defining aspect of their condition.

First, near the end of the play, Willy emerges from one of his reveries into the past with the sudden realization that "nothing's planted." He says, "I don't have a thing in the ground." He rushes off to get some seeds. Biff finds him later outside, late at night, planting the seeds. Of course, the action is emblematic: it's not literal seeds that Willy has neglected to plant, but the seeds of enduring, real values that he realizes only now he has failed to implant in his sons. He has left them no legacy, nothing by which they can bear fruit or make their lives better. The essence of the American Dream has been, since America's founding, after all, the dream of building a foundation from which one's children can build a better life. Willy realizes at this point in the play, if only at a subconscious level, that his children are failures because he has failed to give them a foundation for real success.

Despite this realization, Willy still doesn't quite get it. But Biff does. He says to his brother Happy about their father, "The man don't know who we are!" Then Biff confronts Willy while Willy is outside, madly planting seeds. Biff says to Willy, "We never told the truth for ten minutes in this house!" Biff goes on to tell Willy that Willy had so blown Biff full of "hot air" while he was growing up—the hot air of unrealistic expectations and false illusions—that Biff never understood what was required in order to achieve real success. But now, at last, Biff realizes who he is—and who he is not—and that "all I want is out there, waiting for me the minute I say I know who I am!"

Biff's enlightenment is a good argument that it is he—not Willy—who is the play's tragic hero. Biff has suffered loss—his father, for one—but he has, in accordance with the classical definition of the tragic hero, experienced illumination, too. He recognizes his father's fatal error: following someone else's calling instead of his own.

Unlike Biff's, my own father provided a fitting model for the pursuit of calling. Although I inherited my small mouth and apple-shape, my love of books and animals, and the gift of teaching from my mother, everything else came from my father: my nose, my fair complexion, my love of coffee and newspapers, my quick judgments and analytical thinking, and my tendency to double-check everything.

Just before my family was readying for our move from Maine for my father's job, and I was facing leaving my beloved Monmouth Academy and my best and beloved friend Rachael, my father took me out for lunch at Leone's Pizzeria. My mom had never learned to like pizza or any dishes she hadn't been raised with on the farm, but a more adventurous palate is something else I got from my father. The pizzeria, one of only two eating establishments in our town, had just three booths. Dad and I sat in the middle one next to the window, and over our slices of pepperoni pizza, he asked me how I was coping with the upcoming changes. I don't recall what I answered, but it must have been reassuring because of what he said. My father told me that he thought my oldest brother tended not to take things seriously enough, my other brother tended to take things too seriously, and that I took things just right. These words went a long way for me. I had felt many times in my life like I took things too seriously. But here was the man whose judgment and character I trusted more than anyone I knew saying I had it "just right." And when I knew I was erring in other ways, I carried with me the assurance that I could face the world and shoulder whatever might come. These were freeing, empowering words. Unlike Biff's father Willy, my father was planting the seeds of success in my life.

For 25 years my father worked in middle management for a large industrial textile company. When I was little, he took me to his office on occasion. I would sit in the sparse windowless space with striped brown carpeting, and I would color, wondering what was in all those metal filing cabinets that lined one wall and what exactly was being made in the huge factory at the other end of the building. Once my father took me to visit the company's owner in his big office on the top floor of the plant.

This office was very big with a large picture window looking out over the city. The office smelled like wood and cigars.

One time the boss came to our house for dinner. A few days later, my father brought home a small paper bag, saying it was for me, from the boss. He wanted me to guess what was inside the bag by smelling it, so I sniffed inside.

"It smells like cigars," I announced. But it wasn't cigars. It was a big box of brand new crayons. I put my nose in the bag again. They smelled good.

I never really understood what it was my father did, although he said it was called "customer service." To me he was a business man, and the image I had of him when I was a child was all wrapped up in the suit and tie he wore to work every day. Whatever it was that he was doing, he seemed to take it seriously and to do it well. Once when the company psychiatrist came and interviewed all the managers, my mother told me afterward about how the psychiatrist couldn't understand why my father showed no wish to climb up the corporate ladder. It seemed my father was not only good at what he was doing, but he was content, too, something the company shrink couldn't quite figure out. My dad told my mom not long ago, after he'd retired for good, that all he'd ever wanted in life was a good job and a woman to love—and he'd found both. In so doing, he fulfilled his calling. And taught me about finding and fulfilling mine.

Yet, my father had more to teach me. After he retired from the corporation and moved with my mother to Florida, with a number of solid working years ahead of him, he sought out a second career. He chose to work in a tool shop. No more suit and tie. And, surprisingly to me alone, that seemed to fit him just fine. I had thought the jacket and tie were as much a part of who he is as his curly red hair and his need to read the newspaper every evening.

My father's career change took place soon after I had started college. After I had completed three semesters as a social work major, I walked into the office of the English Department Chair with a form that required his signature permitting me to change my major to English. I had had Dr. Miner for an American Literature survey class during my second semester. He had urged me then to think about majoring in English, but I had told him I would never be an English major because I didn't take English that seriously.

Three semesters, two statistics courses, several sociology and psychology courses (even some extras taken during the summer session), I decided in the middle of exam week, almost on a whim, to drop my social work major and switch to English. It was a serious decision, but not that serious. I had no better reason than simply that in studying books, I felt at home.

When I handed Dr. Miner the form and asked him to sign it there in his small office, smaller even than my father's had been at the company, he reminded me, with a sly smile from behind the stacks of books on his desk, of what I had said about never being an English major. I gladly ate the little slice of humble pie Dr. Miner served me that day, telling him sheepishly that I had changed my mind. What I didn't tell him was that I was pretty certain I had finally discovered who I wasn't—and maybe who I was.

9

The Fate of the Romantic: *Madame Bovary*

We are like sculptors, constantly carving out of
others the image we long for, need, love or desire, often against reality, against their benefit,
and always, in the end, a disappointment, because it does not fit them.

—Anaïs Nin

"But, Susan, I thought this was everything you wanted." I was sitting at the kitchen table in Susan and Duane's modest home, one
filled with as many children as it had rooms. The house was shoe-
horned into the cul-de-sac of a neighborhood of post-World War
II dwellings that had been built by the government to provide af-
fordable homes for returning soldiers but were now inhabited by
lower-middle class homeowners and renters who, unable to escape
to the further suburbs, had settled for straddling the city's edge.

I took another sip of coffee and added, "You know, the husband, the kids, the white picket fence." A child cried in her crib in
the other room. Another busied herself at our feet piling up wooden
blocks and knocking them back down onto the floor. The rest were
at school.

"Oh yeah. I wanted this." Her hand swept across the air,
as though to indicate all that was before us and around us: the av-
ocado-colored Sears Kenmore refrigerator and stove, the empty
baby bottles in the sink, the white plastic shoe rack by the door
overflowing with sneakers of all sizes, the wall hanging made from
a white and blue plaid dishcloth with a cartoon cow stretched
across a wooden frame, and the coat rack in the corner, empty

save a baby sling hanging from it like a noose. "And I still want it," Susan continued. "I'm not gonna leave Duane or anything. I could never do that even if I wanted to." She got up and moved to the sink to begin washing the bottles. "It's no big deal."

While the sink filled with water, she poured the remaining coffee into our cups and immersed the empty carafe into the soapy water. "Duane's the one making a mountain out of molehill," she said, putting her hands into the sink and scrubbing vigorously. "It was just a few phone conversations. It's not like we did anything." She stopped to listen for the crying in the other room, but it had stopped. "I would never do anything." She carefully placed a bottle in the dish drainer. "Even if I did have the guts to. Which I don't," she said.

Susan was a longtime family friend and had been one of the attendants in my wedding just a few weeks before. My parents had known her parents for years, and with our last move had found ourselves close to where Susan lived. Susan was ten years older than I, old enough for me to see her as an experienced elder while young enough to still be sort of cool sometimes. Susan's father was a well-respected scientist, but Susan hadn't wanted even to go to college. Instead, she'd married her high school sweetheart and had five kids before she was thirty.

My parents had helped hers through some rough years of their marriage some years back before I could even remember. Her parents had stayed together, apparently fairly happily, and this formed a kind of unspoken bond among us all. Susan expressed the bond by acting as a surrogate big sister to me. As much as I would let her, anyway. I liked Susan and appreciated her. I liked spending time with her kids, too. But she and I were different, more so than she seemed to see.

Susan was not living happily-ever-after with Duane, her high school sweetheart husband. This was due to no great failure on Duane's part. He was steadily, if modestly, employed, and an attentive husband and father who was very present in the small home they'd been able to buy shortly after the birth of their first and quickly filled to brimming with the rest. Duane was, in fact, the epitome of a decent guy, a little slower than in the heyday of his varsity basketball days, but definitely one of the good guys.

Susan was more tentative. Despite being a stay-at-home mom, she somehow managed to befriend men with whom she would flirt, engage in deep conversations, and even invite to church. If she was honest, sometimes she felt a little in love with them. But because she was a devout Catholic, cheating wasn't an option. In fact, she had confided to me that part of the reason she'd married Duane was because they had slept together—once—before they were married. She felt afterwards that she belonged to him. Forever. Divorce was almost as unthinkable as cheating. Besides, she didn't want a divorce. She didn't even want any of her adventures to cause more than ripples in the smooth surface of her marital bliss. So she tiptoed exhilaratingly close to the boundary between chaste and cheating.

Though hers was the chastest cheating imaginable, it was still cheating to my way of thinking. And apparently, Duane's, too.

I couldn't quite figure out how to advise Susan. After all, it was she who had always played the part in our relationship of the older, wiser dispenser of advice and wisdom, and I the recipient. But even if I had felt freer to advise her, I wasn't sure how.

It seemed like since my own marriage a few weeks before, she'd felt more compelled to share more and more details with me of her escapades past and present. I couldn't tell if her desire to tell was rooted in a spirit of resentment or foreboding, but I was stymied either way. I was sure that my marriage would not fall into such error. On the other hand, I'm sure Susan never would have imagined in her own newlywed days that her dreams of happily-ever-after would degenerate to this.

I believed in "for better or worse"—and had just uttered those very vows myself. But wasn't romance the point of marriage? Or at least a big part? What do you do when the romance is gone? How do you keep your eye and heart from straying? The vows I'd exchanged so recently with my new husband didn't include the phrase "happily ever after." Our traditional wedding ceremony, held at a rural, independent bible church that prohibited dancing at the basement reception we hosted afterward, did include the phrase "for better or worse." I knew that happily-ever-after was the stuff of fairy tales. But if things went from better to worse, were the only options tolerating worse or chaste cheating?

Despite—or perhaps because of—marrying after a brief engagement, within one year of our first date, I never really experienced the pre-wedding jitters. There was a moment, though, alone one night in bed before falling asleep, when I committed to myself no turning back. Lying there in the dark atop my twin mattress on the floor of the small bedroom in the apartment I shared with my college roommates, I committed then—to myself and to God, even before I made my public profession before a community of witnesses at the altar—that I was making this commitment for life. Till death do us part. I tried, lying there in the dark, to think of all the possible things that could cause me in some distant future to regret my decision. Caught in the palm of young earnest love, that was difficult.

Finally, I imagined the worst scene imaginable: falling out of love. I paused and tried as hard as I could to imagine what that might be like. Even then, I vowed, I am committing myself to this, mind, heart, and soul. Not only to him and to me but to our marriage. I sensed that I would fail myself. Perhaps he might fail me in some way, too. But the marriage was a third entity—a holy entity—that required that commitment I pledged in the dark. I hadn't been talking to God much in recent years, but I asked him that night to be with me. And with us. It was the first time I had truly put myself—utterly, entirely, and completely—into the hands of God.

Some months later, married just weeks, I felt a little bit wiser. My new husband and I had had our first big blow-up the day after returning from our brief honeymoon in the snowy Pocono Mountains. I did wonder how hard it would be—not now, of course, but in years to come—to forsake all others. The new busboy at the Howard Johnson where I was now working part-time while finishing up school was so cute and funny that it was hard not to notice and to wonder if we'd might have had a chance if I were unattached. But I still didn't really understand what Susan was going through. What she was putting herself through. I just didn't know what to say to Susan.

But Gustave Flaubert might have.

My world literature professor introduced me to Flaubert, and more to the point, his masterpiece *Madame Bovary*. I had no idea when my professor assigned it to us that my entire worldview was about to change.

Emma Bovary, of the title, is a wistful romantic, the daughter of a modest country farmer who had, before the novel opens, sent his only child to a convent, as was common enough within rural farm families. Emma's time at the convent cultivated within her a taste for sensory experience, mystery, and drama. Flaubert depicts the ancient Catholic faith as complicit in developing Emma's romantic spirit: "When she went to confession, she invented little sins in order that she might stay there longer, kneeling in the shadow, her hands joined, her face against the grating beneath the whispering of the priest." Having come from a quiet simple life on her father's farm, Emma develops a taste for the melodramatic. "Accustomed to the quieter aspects of life, she turned instead to its tumultuous parts. She loved the sea only for the sake of its storms, and the green only when it was scattered among ruins."

Such sentimentality—an indulgence in emotion for emotion's sake—is paralleled by Milan Kundera in another novel, *The Unbearable Lightness of Being*, in a passage about kitsch, or sentimental art:

> Kitsch causes two tears to flow in quick succession. The first tear says: How nice to see children running on the grass! The second tear says: How nice to be moved, together with all mankind, by children running on the grass! It is the second tear that makes kitsch kitsch.

Likewise, Emma luxuriates in emotion as an end in itself. She takes pride in her heightened sensibilities and her propensity toward the dramatic. In feeling great grief at her mother's death, "Emma was secretly pleased that she had reached at a first attempt the rare ideal of delicate lives, never attained by mediocre hearts." The woman who will soon become *Madame Bovary* thinks herself unique and set apart from common humanity. One of many clever ironies the author inserts into the narrative is that there are actually three women in the story named Madame Bovary: Emma, her husband's first wife, and his mother. Emma's mistaken sense of herself as unique rather than human is her tragic flaw.

Emma's schooling in romantic sentimentalism came—ironically enough, like my own education—through books. But these were different books. The convent's maid provided her with tantalizing novels that fed Emma's growing hunger for romance over life. These books,

> were all about love, lovers, sweethearts, persecuted ladies fainting in lonely pavilions, postilions killed at every relay, horses ridden to death on every page, somber forests, heart-aches, vows, sobs, tears and kisses, little boat rides by moonlight, nightingales in shady groves, gentlemen brave as lions, gentle as lambs, virtuous as no one ever was, always well dressed, and weeping like fountains.

"I have come to love stories that move breathlessly along, that frighten one," she declares. "I detest commonplace heroes and moderate feelings, as one finds them in nature."

To detest people and things as they are found "in nature," in their real state, is to reject nothing less than life itself, as Emma's story will bear out. Yes, moments of transcendence and glimpses of the divine are real. But their rarity is their significance. Life is grounded in the mundane. But the mundane has a bad rap. The word simply means "world"; its origins are shared with the same root word for "mountain." On the other hand, the world of ideals— meaning "forms" in the language of that premiere idealist, Plato— is up there, out there, somewhere. The world of the mundane is here and now and is not to be rejected but to be loved. Just as people are to be loved for who they are, imperfections and all, not the versions of them we make in our own image. Including husbands and wives. Especially husbands and wives.

I was a romantic and didn't know it. It's not that I expected a

knight in shining armor to come sweep me off my feet. Not a literal one, anyway. But each age has its own version of knights and
the women who fall under the fantasy's spell. The Lancelot of the
Middle Ages became the Romeo of the Renaissance, the Heath-
cliff of the Romantic age, Prince Albert of the Victorian age, and
James Dean of the twentieth century. When I was growing up, any
one of a plethora of celebrities who were famous enough to grace
the pages of *Tiger Beat* and be blown up on a glossy poster for
hanging in a girl's room would do. But all the types boiled down
to this: a man who would sweep you away, be steadfast and faithful, and, of course, make all the other girls jealous. I wrote stories
and poems with passionate lovers, self-destructive protagonists,
murderous revenge, and intensely natural surroundings.

In high school, my favorite author was the arch-Romantic
William Blake. In Senior English, I did a lengthy research paper on
him and got an A. When I switched my major to English in college, I did so under the illusion that all good literature is about
mystery, passion, nature, and feelings. When one of my professors invited the class over to his house, I was surprised to find that
he lived in the city. As far as I know, all of my English professors
did. I had thought all literary types lived close to nature.

Sometimes what looks like romanticism is just immaturity.
It can be hard to tell the difference. In ninth grade when my friend
Rachael was dating a senior named Thomas, Thomas and a friend
stopped by my house once when Rachael and I were there. His friend
was interested in me, but the feeling wasn't mutual, in no small
part because his family farmed pigs. Not the industrial kind, just
old-fashioned country pig farmers. Either way, it wasn't cool.

It was summer and we enjoyed just hanging out. We wandered
around outside and came upon the raspberry patch. We began to
pick them to eat, but soon Thomas and his friend were in the middle of a berry-throwing battle. As things heated up, the boys took
off their shirts. The raspberries flew, and eventually one landed
with what seemed to be an audible *plop* in the middle of Thomas's
bare chest, hairless and white. The raspberry stuck there for what
seemed like an eternity before rolling clumsily down. Rachael and
I exchanged scornful looks. I knew exactly what Rachael was

thinking.

She had been tiring of Thomas. This would be it. The awkwardness of the moment, its utter uncoolness, was doom. There was no shaking the image of that broken and bleeding raspberry stuck on Thomas' pale flesh. Rachael broke up with Thomas a few days later after he wiped out riding his bicycle. I don't recall the explanation she gave him, but we both knew it was because the real Thomas had replaced the fantasy Thomas. The fantasy Thomas would never look as silly as the real one had covered in fruit. The dream had flopped like that fresh raspberry hurled onto soft, white flesh.

We knew, Rachael and I, that it was wrong. We knew we were being shallow and superficial. Somewhere in our heads we knew it was wrong to judge a person and a relationship this way, to judge it for being too real, although we didn't really know why it was wrong. No one was telling us about romanticism and realism. Besides, we were fifteen, and we couldn't get our feelings to match up with our brains. So we went with our feelings.

For a long time, that's how I thought it was to be: feelings as the measure of love. Excitement. Pleasure. Approval. Smoothness, not awkwardness. I was no different from other girls in this respect. Conditioned by popular culture, movies, television, and even many lesser books, I had come, like most young girls, to expect love to be something more like balloons in the air than daisies in the ground.

Such romanticism isn't limited to silly teenage girls. Romanticism is a form of idealism. Real relationships are grounded in life. Not the kind of idealism that hopes for the best, but rather one that refuses to see and accept reality. Idealism sees the world in terms of extremes: good/bad, black/white, ugly/beautiful. The old cowboy Westerns, a genre of romance, don't have any cowboys in gray; they all don either black hats or white. The same for that more modern romance, *Star Wars*. And, of course, in the original romances, centered on the Arthurian legends of the Knights of the Round Table, the men were either gallants or giants, and the women either damsels in distress or crones. Some women were both—not at the same time, but one or the other until some magic revealed their true identity, like the beast in *Beauty and the Beast*.

The most common modern romances are the Harlequin kind. And even more recent versions of these stories—those that add vampires or eroticism of other twists—are simply variations of the same old formula in which a man rescues a woman (if only from herself), and she transforms him in return. A sure recipe for disaster when such expectations are carried over into real life.

These ideals don't leave much room for nuance. Real people are neither entirely good nor entirely bad, entirely beautiful nor entirely ugly, neither perfect heroes nor dastardly villains. Real people are a mixture. Admittedly, many of us have certain types we are attracted to. But "type" is just another word for "ideal." Categorizing someone according to a type requires whittling out the idiosyncrasies of a person in order to fit into the designated mold. But smoothing out the edges only makes one dull. I never realized I was guilty of doing this to my own husband until a year or two after we were married.

We had travelled back to Maine for a visit. I was able to catch up with Rachael; we'd kept up our friendship even after I'd moved away the year after the raspberry patch incident. I brought pictures and excitedly got her up to date on my new married life.

"Well, you did it!" she said when I finally stopped to take a breath, giving Rachael a chance to get a word in.

"Did what?" I asked.

"You married a rock star." she answered.

I looked at her quizzically. I didn't know what she was talking about.

"You always used to say when we were teenagers that you wanted to marry a rock star. And you did."

I was mortified, but tried not to let it show. I hadn't even remembered that. But now that she had reminded me, I realized it was true. Had I really married him because he was a rock star? Suddenly, I felt like a sham.

My husband was not a "rock star." He was a person. A person who was thoughtful and kind and smart and talented and funny and cute. And, yes, who played the guitar. Yes, he had been in a band when we met. And when we married. In fact, he had caught my attention for the very first time when my friend Tina and I teetered on high heels and tight jeans into the club that last Friday night of the semester and headed straight for the stage. I eyed him from across the room and walked closer and stood there until we made eye contact. When the band took a break some numbers later, Tina and I meandered through the crowd and ended up by the entrance to the band's dressing room. We decided to hang out there for a while. Tina had her eye on the bassist. It worked. By the end of the night, Tina had given her phone number to the bassist, and a month later when the band returned to the club and we showed up, the guitarist left with mine.

One year later to the day was our wedding.

I was two months shy of my 20th birthday. We had both come out of painful relationships in which we had been the injured parties. I was still in college, and neither of us had stable employment. He was on the road travelling with the band. I was waitressing at Howard Johnson's the hours I was off from school. "We can be poor together or poor apart," we thought, rather romantically. We chose together.

Our first apartment was a little one bedroom unit added onto a stately old home that the owner had turned into an antique shop. It sat snugly in the hollow of a suburban village about a half hour from my school. The apartment was equipped with an antique porcelain stove, one large kitchen/dining/living area, and lovely hardwood floors throughout. Most of the windows looked out into a large yard that backed up to a low stone wall. Our landlady ran the antique shop and lived upstairs with her bachelor son, an artist who flitted back and forth between there and New York City. The landlady was about five feet tall with silver hair and bright lipstick and wore lacy vintage dresses, usually black. She had told us no pets were allowed, but easily gave in when I brought an English Springer Spaniel home "just to try out for the weekend." Yes, our marriage had a romantic, storybook beginning.

I know what's supposed to happen next in a good story is some terrible or devastating conflict: the discovery that one of us had a rare cancer, maybe, or the reemergence of an old flame whose heart was full of wicked intent. But that's not what happened, although we did argue a lot about the dog. What happened is that we returned from our short honeymoon in time for me to start the spring semester, the term I opened the pages of *Madame Bovary.*

Unfortunately, Emma's education, particularly the books she read, whetted her appetite for romance and not life. When she meets Charles—and then Leon, followed by Rodolphe—she mistakes excitement for love.

Having returned to her father's home from the convent, having no other prospects for the future before her, and possessing no experience but that which she'd gained vicariously through books, Emma readily assents to her father's desire for her to marry the widowed doctor, Charles Bovary, who'd cared for his broken leg. Charles, however, is nothing like the dashing heroes of Emma's books. Charles, in fact, was awkward and dull and, as it turns out, not a highly skilled doctor. But he adored Emma.

Emma thinks perhaps the feeling is mutual. This is quickly shown not to be so, however. "Before marriage," the narrator says,

> she thought herself in love; but since the happiness that should have followed her failed to come, she must, she thought, have been mistaken. And Emma tried to find out what one meant exactly in life by the words bliss, passion, ecstasy, that had seemed to her so beautiful in books.

But it is not only Charles that disappoints her. Everything about her new life is disappointing. Nothing in the world away from her father's country farm is like the world of her books. Even her new name, "Madame Bovary," is second hand: because Charles is a widower she is the second Madame Bovary, or rather, the third because Charles's mother still hovers. Even during the honeymoon, which Emma tries to enjoy, she wonders,

> Why could not she lean over balconies in Swiss chalets, or enshrine her melancholy in a Scotch cottage, with a husband dressed in a black velvet coat with long tails, and thin shoes, a pointed hat

and frills?…. And yet, in accord with theories she believed right, she wanted to experience love with him. By moonlight in the garden she recited all the passionate rhymes she knew by heart, and, sighing, sang to him many melancholy adagios; but she found herself as calm after this as before, and Charles seemed neither more amorous, nor more moved.

If she were able to express her discontentment perhaps she might have overcome it. Indeed she thinks that if Charles could only understand her, even if only in part, her heart might yield "a sudden bounty." But she does not have the words to express her yearnings and disappointments. Unreleased, they simmer. As the intimacy of married life with her husband deepens, "the greater became the gulf that kept them apart." For intimacy with Charles reveals that the doctor who successfully treated her father's bone fracture—the occasion of Emma and Charles' meeting—is, in fact, a man, and a rather ordinary, dull, and flawed one at that.

The fact that no man is able to satisfy Emma reveals that even if Charles had been a bit less, or even a lot less, dull, it would not have been enough. Emma's discovery that her husband is a real person, not just an image, is a discovery most of us must undertake. And it's a discovery that is made not just once and for all, but—particularly within the context of marriage—over and over, sometimes on a daily basis, as I had to learn for myself.

Upon returning home from our honeymoon, we learned that my husband's band (which was also his full-time employment) was breaking up. Two of the band members were sleeping together and the husband of one of them found out. That was the end of that—the band, that is.

A week later, we got into our first big fight. Really big. Loud. Nasty. Tearful and sleepless. It was—predictably—over money. While I had blissfully closed my eyes to the obviously rapid spending going on in the whirl of setting up house, wedding, and honeymoon, I had the nerve only a newlywed can boast to accuse my husband of deceiving me about our financial situation. Even worse than making the accusation was fooling myself into believing it to be true. The honeymoon had waxed and was now waned.

Suddenly unemployed, my husband got to work looking for a job. Steady work in the music industry wasn't easy to come by, so while he did auditions here and there, he knew he needed to find other work, fast. I was headed back to school and we couldn't live long on my twenty hours a week of waitressing at Howard Johnson's. So he cut his long, beautiful hair short and, after a couple of false starts, started his own business and worked to support us while I finished college. And then graduate school. And then more graduate school.

We underwent a lot of changes in those first few weeks and months. And more, naturally, over the years. It's true of most couples, I suspect, particularly of young ones like us in the fresh stage of love as we were to fool ourselves and the other into being what we think—often mistakenly—the other wants us to be, or even more likely, what we think we should be to and for the other person. We both had expectations about the other, about the person we had married and committed the rest of our lives to. And I think it's fair to say that some of those expectations were shown to be false over time. And true, too.

There were numerous revelations: I had tried to convince myself that I enjoyed playing volleyball because it was something we could do together. It lasted only as long I could go without getting hit on the head really, really hard. Which wasn't very long. And he, in turn, went horseback riding with me a few times because it was something I loved to do. He still likes to tell the story of his first (and last) gallop, undertaken quite unexpectedly when our trail leader suddenly announced to the train of riders behind her, "Let's run!"

Of the two of us, I proved to be the greater changeling. I had presented myself—because it's what I thought I was—as a doting, domestic, and conventional wife. I don't know for sure if my husband thought he was marrying someone who would cook and bake and support him in his career, but that's what I had thought I would do. Both of us came from families based on that model. And I tried. Really I did. Because I thought that was not only what he wanted, but what I wanted to. When he started his own business and we went to an accountant to set up the books, everyone assumed that I'd be the one doing the bookkeeping and phone calls. But I was in school during business hours. Even more to the point, I was an English major. How was I supposed to do accounting?

I couldn't keep accounts, but I could argue. I undertook a disagreement, large or small, in the same way I'd tackle a paper for class: with research, dissection, documentation, and expert wordsmithing. My arguments with my husband were like the work of a detached surgeon: the patient was lost, but the operation was a success.

Those were some trying challenges not only to our marriage but to our sense of ourselves and the other person. It seemed like the false images we had of each other came as much from outside as from ourselves or each other—from popular songs, from romantic movies, and from adolescent whispers. Filled with such ideas, we entered marriage bearing false witness against one another.

I suppose this is true for most everyone. It was certainly true for Emma Bovary. Perhaps if someone had told her that the stories she read in those romance novels were only stories and not reflective of life, perhaps she might have been saved. But no one told her. They only told her to stop reading the books.

But it was too late. If the right books can save your soul, then perhaps the wrong ones can damn it.

By reading these books, the narrator informs us, Emma developed a "veneration for illustrious or unhappy women," unwittingly setting herself up to become one of the latter. How could it be otherwise when she rejects life as it is in favor of life as she wishes it to be? Throughout the novel, Emma is often depicted as standing at a window, forehead pressed against the glass, looking out at the world. This characteristic stance expresses Emma's attitude toward life, boredom and distance, which reinforce one another inevitably, something she cannot see. Her boredom with life causes her to withdraw, but in withdrawing from life in search of an illusory dream, she is destined for the ennui, or weariness with the world, that propels her onto her self-destructive path. When she and her new husband arrive for the first time to their new home she wonders dreamily what would happen to her bridal bouquet if she were to die. This is, of course, foreshadowing. But it also illustrates Emma's refusal to embrace life. Frequently, her eyes are described as "half-closed," the posture of willful blindness and denial—and usually, in both literature and life, the precursor to tragedy.

Charles, in contrast, takes immense pleasure in the ordinary, everyday things. He embraces the tangible concreteness of life:

> He was happy then, and without a care in the world. A meal together, a walk in the evening on the highroad, a gesture of her hands over [Emma's] hair, the sight of her straw hat hanging from the window-fastener, and many other things of which he had never suspected how pleasant they could be, now made up the endless round of his happiness.

While Emma daydreams about her former days in the convent, about Paris, about dying, Charles "trotted over the country roads in snow and rain. He ate omelets on farmhouse tables, poked his arm into damp beds, received the tepid spurt of blood-letting in his face, listened to death-rattles, examined basins, turned over a good deal of dirty linen" and enjoyed each evening a ready dinner and a blazing fire, basking in Emma's company. Yes, Charles is awkward and dull. The novel paints him clearly as a character not to be admired. But, nor is he to be despised. He takes pleasure in life. And in his wife. Perhaps if Emma had done the same, he might have come to be less awkward and dull.

Emma is disenchanted with everything. She hates provincial life. She dreams of the glamorous lives she encounters at a ball she and Charles are invited to attend. As the ordinariness of their lives continues, Emma sinks deeper into a monotony-wrought despair. She keeps "waiting in her heart for something to happen," something of excitement to fulfill her longing, her unbearable heaviness of being. Most torturous is dinner time with her husband. Emma's anorexic soul recoils at the common pleasure of fellowship around a meal. The very things that make us human are too mundane for Emma.

Such dissatisfaction with life renders Emma unable to cope with failure and disappointment, even in herself. One great disappointment is that the child she bears is a girl, not a boy. Upon Charles' excited cry, "It is a girl!" the narrator writes, "She turned her head away and fainted." Motherhood makes her wax hot or cold. She doesn't enjoy it and then, feeling guilty, tries to compensate with a frenetic rush of mothering that alleviates neither the neglected child nor her. Likewise, when a mutual attraction develops between her and Leon, a law clerk living in her small town, rather than face her feelings honestly, Emma plunges herself into mothering, desperately trying to fool herself rather than face reality. Such denial of her human weaknesses and desires only makes her more vulnerable. Vulnerability is romanticism's first tool. By the time a wealthy rake targets Emma for seduction, she is ripe for the taking.

Her seducer, Rodolphe, a client of Charles's, seizes his chance to pursue Emma at the town's Agricultural Fair, a backdrop that Flaubert exploits ingeniously to showcase the art of his realism. As Emma and Rodolphe stroll hand-in-hand along the fairgrounds exchanging impassioned confessions to one another, the narrator intersperses their high talk with the voice of the fair announcer behind them, declaring prizes such as the one "for manures!" As they swear not to forget one another, to think of the other always, the announcer behind them drones, "Hog! First prize equally divided between Messrs. Lehrisse and Cullembourg, sixty francs!" And so the scene goes, for some length, the irony of the earthiness surrounding their idealism completely escaping the soon-to-be-lovers caught in the web of their romanticism.

When the affair is consummated not long thereafter, Emma returns home, gazes at herself in the mirror and repeats, "I have a lover! A lover!" It is just as in the books she has read.

> Then she recalled the heroines of the books that
> she had read, and the lyric legion of these adul-

terous women began to sing in her memory with the voice of sisters that charmed her. She became herself, as it were, an actual part of these lyrical imaginings; at long last, as she saw herself among those lovers she had so envied, she fulfilled the love-dream of her youth.

She is now living the tale. Her dreams have come true.

Then two crises in Emma's life occur in rapid succession, each a harsh intrusion of reality to which her response is only to heighten her attempts to escape ordinary life. First, an operation on which she and Charles had pinned the hopes of success that would lead to widespread fame fails disastrously. Emma's bitterness and disappointment in her husband redoubles and she turns with increased desperation to her lover. Having mistaken her lover's dalliance with her for real love, she exhorts him to run away with her. He agrees outwardly, but secretly has no intention of permanently entangling himself in a complicated relationship with a woman he meant only as a means of temporary diversion. So instead of arriving according to the rendezvous he pretended to agree to, he sends her a letter of false regret.

Above the signature is the mundane closing, "Your friend."

The rest of the novel depicts Emma's continued attempts at escaping ennui—that consuming boredom—of a life that cannot match the world as she fantasizes it to be. Erroneously thinking her boredom comes from outside herself, she takes another lover, establishes a secret life with him in the city, only to become bored with her second lover, then runs herself and Charles into debt in buying needless luxuries that she hopes will make her life extraordinary.

Yet, she still fails to learn to take pleasure in the real world. Even in the midst of her first romantic infatuation, the narrator tells us that she prefers to "delight in his image" in solitude than to be in his actual company. "Emma thrilled at the sound of his step; then in his presence the emotion subsided…" Emma prefers the idea to the reality.

When she makes her final attempt at escape, it's fatal. Even this she fails to see—until it's too late—for what it is. After she has ingested the arsenic she obtains by tricking the unwitting pharmacist's helper, she lies down and thinks, "Ah! It is but a little thing, death! I shall fall asleep and all will be over."

But it is not so.

Emma's death is anything but romantic, and in the spirit of realism, Flaubert spares few of the ugly, realistic details.

There is one moment in Emma's seemingly endless dying that almost escapes the reader amidst the swells of her agony. It is, perhaps, the most important in the entire work. During the endless hours of her dying, Charles tries desperately to save her life and to comfort her. In the midst of this, before Emma loses her wits entirely, the narrator relates that Charles looks upon her "with a tenderness in his eyes such as she had never seen." Other translations of the work render tenderness as love, which makes the point even clearer: the romance, and more importantly, the true love Emma had been searching for had been hers for the taking all along. If only she had opened her eyes to see it.

Emma Bovary's story is about what happens to a woman who builds a life around false images and undergoes the inevitable disappointments for doing so. My story about *Madame Bovary* is about what didn't happen. *Madame Bovary* prevented me from cheating. I don't mean I would have taken a lover if I'd not been warned by her story in time. Although, who knows? Maybe I would have. It's not so dramatic as that. There was no near-lover waiting one night for me in a dew dripped garden under a swelling moon, to whom at the last minute I sent a letter or text message, calling it all off.

The truth is more subtle.

In seeing Emma, I simply saw myself. I sought excitement. I thought love meant eternal excitement and unfluctuating passion. I didn't recognize my romanticism for what it was: discontentment with what is, caused by pining for what isn't. I didn't know the difference between a real person and my idealized version of a person. *Madame Bovary* changed my worldview. It made me realize that happiness is in here, not out there. That the imperfect love of a real person is far greater than the perfect love that exists only in fairy tales or movies. That living happily-ever-after begins with embracing life—not fleeing to fantasies—today.

We all have people in our lives who see us only at our best, in narrow one-dimensional slivers that distort our images to our advantage: talented colleague, witty friend, organized committee member. Such relationships project ideal versions of facets of ourselves that leave out the weak, ugly stuff. I can understand the appeal to the businessman of an affair with a young underling at work. Such people, whose job it is to attend and flatter, become like trick department store mirrors, the kind that reflect a more flattering, but false, image of yourself, an image that is seen only in front of that mirror and only by you and no one else.

Similarly, one of the greatest occupational hazards in being a professor is being surrounded all day by people who are rewarded for listening to you and who, from time to time, come to adore you. Even if you have no desire to develop a romantic relationship, it's still not easy to make the daily transition back to the world at home where not every word you speak is taken in like pure oxygen, where in fact you have very little expertise, a fact that is shown every time you grumble inarticulately, or forget how not to flood the lawn mower engine, or burn the pancakes on the second side. It's hard sometimes to transform from queen—or rock star— to mere mortal. But it is always to a mere mortal, and as a mere mortal, that we choose to be faithful or not.

A longtime friend who has been married almost as long as I have and who had a lot of tough things to work out in her marriage relationship once told me that the thing she admires most about my marriage is that we accept one another for who we are; we don't try to change each other. I think that's owing, at least in part, to *Madame Bovary*.

After we finished reading the book in my class, I called Susan. "You have to read this book," I said. "You just have to." I really thought it would help her see what I could now see, that it would help her to take joy in what she had—Duane, the kids, the house, the slice of lawn, the wall hanging made from a dish towel. It might not all have been the stuff of dreams. It was far from perfect. But it was real.

I went out and bought a paperback copy of the book and

brought it over to Susan. "Thanks," she said. It was Saturday and the kids were swirling around, so I didn't add anything more to what I'd said over the phone except, simply, "Please read it."

For several months I kept asking Susan if she was reading it and always got some sort of excuse. Eventually, I noticed the book had been placed behind the glass door of her good bookcase where I continued to spot it for years to come. Susan never read it. Eventually, my husband and I moved to another state. Susan and Duane are still together. I don't know if they are happy.

10

Real Love is Like a Compass: John Donne's Metaphysical Poetry

so much depends
upon
a red wheel
barrow
glazed with rain
water
beside the white
chickens.

—William Carlos Williams,
    "The Red Wheel Barrow"

One Christmas morning, after all the gifts had been opened, my husband announced that there was one more present in the garage, one that wouldn't fit under the tree. When it comes to gifts, my husband is both creative and generous, so I don't even try to guess any more. I never would have guessed what this present was: a wheelbarrow.

It was perfect.

I know. A wheelbarrow doesn't sound like the perfect present from anyone, let alone from a husband to his wife on Christmas morning. Oh, but this was no ordinary wheelbarrow. It boasted double wheels in the front, making it harder to accidentally tip over, and an extra-large green bucket made of strong polymer light enough that I could cart it around even with a full load. All in all, it was a deluxe, state-of-the-art wheelbarrow, the sort of luxury I'd never have bought for myself.

Many years of marriage means many birthdays, anniversaries,

and other obligatory gift days. Finding a perfect (or even decent) present to give a spouse on each of these events, over and over again, is one of the never-talked-about challenges of marriage life. My husband had learned early on, the hard way, that kitchen appliances just wouldn't do unless requested. What I loved so much about the wheelbarrow (besides its sheer utility) is that it was something that required a certain amount of knowing me, knowing my daily life and needs, knowing the pleasure I take in caring for the horses and chickens each day, in order to see its fittingness. Having already had a perfectly usable, if far inferior, wheelbarrow, I certainly didn't need a new one. And it would have been easier, in both conception and execution, to buy me a necklace or jacket or such. The wheelbarrow was a gift chosen because it was perfect for me.

We spent a few minutes, there in the garage, examining the wheelbarrow's deluxe features while he told me the story of how he'd come upon it. The best presents often come with stories. Before taking the bright, clean new vessel out to the horse barn where its virgin state would irreversibly alter, he urged me to climb into the big basin, and I did. He wheeled me around our driveway, just as a rare southern snow began to spit from the sky. We laughed, I in my pajamas and a furry winter hat, he trotting behind me in heavy work boots, as tiny, white crystals floated around us.

We had been married many years by this morning. I had come to see that lasting love is less like a dinner with candlelight and red roses and more like a wheelbarrow given on Christmas morning. Or like a compass.

A compass, of all things, is what John Donne, the seventeenth century priest and poet, used to describe the love he shared with his wife Anne. Donne, who was Catholic, secretly married Anne, a Protestant, when she was just seventeen. When Anne's powerful father found out, he had Donne imprisoned for weeks. Donne lost his post in Parliament, his political career was ruined, and the couple lived in poverty for the next ten years. Later, he wittily summarized the events this way: John Donne, Anne Donne, Un-Done. Reconciliation with his wife's family eventually came, however. So, too, did Donne's reluctant taking of holy orders in the Anglican Church where he found a new career and success as a clergyman. Anne bore twelve children in sixteen years of marriage, and died of the last one. Donne was inconsolable. He continued to write sermons and devotional poetry, but he wrote love poetry no more.

One of Donne's love poems to his wife is "A Valediction: Forbidding Mourning." It is one of the most passionate love poems in the English language.

Yes, *Madame Bovary* warned me of the dangers of romanticism. But romanticism and passion are not the same. The idealism of romanticism certainly includes strong passion. But passion is much more than romance. Passion has two meanings: suffering and enduring. The first meaning is the one associated with romantic love. It's the passion emanating from desire, a desire whose source lies in the pursuit itself and wanes once the object of desire is obtained. This is why romances, comedies, and novels traditionally end with the wedding: the object of love has been conquered and whatever follows is insignificant to the story.

But the other aspect of passion, one that is all but forgotten is endurance. The word *endure* has come to have primarily negative connotations, but this should not be. Something that is durable is of high quality. It continues to exist through the passage of time. It is good and to be valued. A love that cannot endure is no love at all. Real love—and true passion—endures. And it endures much. It is based on more than fleeting feelings or a desire that is subject to passing moods, fancies, and appetites. It is guided by reason because reason knows what feelings often do not.

Passion wedded to reason—a rare marriage indeed—makes the love described in "A Valediction Forbidding Mourning" transcendent. Donne's view of love, as expressed in this poem and throughout his works, exceeds the formulaic boundaries of romanticism, in which love exists only in the ideal and dissipates upon its manifestation in the real. In contrast, for Donne, love does not founder in the ground of the real, but rather takes root, opens up and flourishes into infinite possibilities that defy the old formulas.

Hence the "realness" of the compass—a useful tool that operates according to the laws of science and has no link to romantic love—provides a fitting, if ingenious, comparison. What the metaphor reveals about a certain kind of love is profound, as one based in firmness, justness, perfection in the sense of completeness not freedom from flaws.

Seldom does one find reason and passion in as perfect balance as one finds in John Donne—in both his poetry and his life. Donne wrote some of the most honest and powerful devotional works ever written. "Batter my heart, three-person'd God .... and bend your force to break, blow, burn and make me new," he implores in one of his most famous poems. In another, he chastens Death itself: "Death, be not proud though some have called thee /Mighty and dreadful, for thou art not so ..." Yet, this same man penned highly erotic poetry, too. At first glance, it seems contradictory, this pious priest writing deeply devotional works, on the one hand, and sly, sexual poems, on the other. But Donne rejects the boundaries wrought by human systems. Donne recognizes that the sexual is spiritual, the religious is physical, and the transcendent is as much a part of reality as the material realm. After all, he was a man whose physical body was placed in prison for his passionate love and his religious faith. For him, *being* encompasses the immaterial as much as the material.

Typically, reason and passion are seen as at odds with one another. But, as Donne reveals in this poem and in the body of his works, in their deepest forms, the two are inextricable. It's a paradox. And paradox is at the heart of the conceit. It is also at the heart of God's relationship with humankind and at the heart of the marriage relationship.

It seems most fitting that a marriage based on genuine love reflects the character of the God who gave us marriage. God's character reveals passion in that he is longsuffering. And Christ is said in the gospels to have felt compassion for others. God's character displays reason in his righteousness and justice, and in the orderliness of creation. Marriage is meant to be rooted in both passion and reason. Many of us, however, tend to err toward either reason or passion, one at the expense of the other, whether in our personal leanings or in our relationships, most of all in marriage.

The marriage of my friends Marianne and Marc was nothing if not passionate. They met while they were students at Columbia University. She was pre-med; he was an art major. Marc's family was French, and all the way through college he lived in both the U. S. and France. Marc is the stereotypical Frenchman—swarthy, swaggering, and sweet. It's no wonder that Marianne—whose own striking beauty hints of the exotic—fell for Marc immediately. They were married before Marianne finished college. Their first child was born within a year, followed by another, then another, another, and one more. All the while, Marianne plugged away at medical school, internship, residency, and, finally, her MD.

Marc painted. Sometimes. He sold a few pieces here and there, now and then, enough to bring in a decent income. But he was temperamental. Some would say abusive. Likely clinical. For years their friends and family tried to reason with either one or the other or both about getting help of some kind, counseling, couples therapy, medication, whatever, at least for the sake of the children. And they did.

They tried. Or at least Marianne did. But with Marc, for various causes known and unknown, there was no reasoning. Yet, even when the kids weren't enough to keep Marc and Marianne together, their mutual passion did. For many, many years. But, eventually, even that was not enough. They divorced. Still they burn for one another.

On the other hand, Lynne and Thomas have been married for over 20 years. They both completed their MBAs and married after meeting at the financial company where they both still work. Without any great efforts either way, they never had children, which is probably a good and natural thing given that they don't seem to like one another very much. Their mutual dislike grew enough over the years that they seriously considered divorce a few years ago. But it didn't seem worth the bother. Neither wanted to give up their rent-controlled apartment, which was spacious enough for separate sleeping quarters, and it would have been hard to figure out which one of them got which cat. They couldn't find a reason to stay together—but they couldn't find any real reason to live apart either. So they chose the most reasonable (and easiest) course and stayed together, no more happily, I think, than before. They seem to have settled into an amicable relationship in their middle stage of life and seemed determined to stay the course. But passion? No, it never was nor is there. The dryness of their marriage has caused each of them to shrivel, making both more brittle to the point that daily life together is a series of small shatterings.

And John and Anne Donne? "If they be two," Donne wrote of his and Anne's souls in "A Valediction: Forbidding Mourning," "they are two so / As stiff twin compasses are two." Comparing one's love to a geometric gadget doesn't sound passionate. It certainly doesn't fit the formulas, but John Donne is nothing if not an unusual poet. The small group of seventeenth century English poets with whom he is associated is called the Metaphysical Poets. They were named such because they wedded matters of eternal and spiritual transcendence to the earthly and temporal. In contrast to the Romantics, who preferred the ideal over the real and the spiritual over the physical, the metaphysical school of poets— among whom John Donne was foremost—recognized these realms as distinct but inseparable. Since such a view is more nuanced than the more black-and-white thinking of romanticism, metaphysical poetry is, not surprisingly, rich and complex—and full of wit.

No wonder that the signature literary device of these poets is called a *conceit*. The conceit is an elaborate metaphor that compares two very unlike things (like love and a compass or, as in another of Donne's poems, sex and a flea bite) in order to draw out an unseen truth by drawing a surprising similarity. The metaphysical conceit does even more than that; its unlikely metaphors link the physical and temporal realm with the spiritual and eternal realm. Thus the metaphysical conceit embodies the notion of the inseparability of the seemingly antithetical realms of the earthly and the transcendent.

Marriage, too, does this. It's a physical manifestation of a spiritual reality: by becoming "one flesh" two differently formed bodies are joined physically and spiritually. Donne illustrates this connection of the material with the immaterial with a compass.

The compass is the culminating conceit in Donne's "A Vale-diction: Forbidding Mourning," but the poet kindly warms us up to the idea with some smaller conceits. Written to his wife on the occasion of the poet's impending departure for what would turn out to be a months-long business trip abroad, he compares their long but temporary separation, first, to a virtuous death, then to the harmless vibration of the concentric spheres of universe, then to malleable gold which can be hammered to thinness without breaking apart. Each of the images conjures a view of love that is both physical and spiritual, both earthly and transcendent—and for all this, both holy and rare.

Then comes the most ingenious of the poem's conceits: the comparison of their love to the twin legs of a compass. "Thy soul," the poet declares to his love, is "the fixed foot," which

> makes no show
> To move, but doth, if the other do;
> And though it in the center sit,
>   Yet when the other far doth roam,
> It leans, and hearkens after it,
>   And grows erect, as that comes home.

Like the two parts of a compass, Donne and his wife are separate, yet unified, in both their physical movements and in their "hear-kening." The poem then continues in a vein anticipatory of his eventual return home at the end of his journey and closes with a final stanza that elaborates and consummates this unexpected comparison of their holy union to that of the compass:

> Such wilt thou be to me, who must,
>   Like the other foot, obliquely run;
> Thy firmness makes my circle just,
>   And makes me end where I begun.

Here the work of a simple mechanical object, a compass, and the profound, abstract notion of justness (or perfection) allows us to witness the infinity and perfection represented in the figure of the circle. It's a picture of the kind of love the poet shares with his wife, but it's also a picture of a metaphysical truth: the physical ushers us into the spiritual.

Marriage is, in this way, metaphysical.

*

God used marriage to gentle me.

For a long time, too long, I couldn't seem to reconcile my ideas of who God was, who I was, and how those two things should shape the life I lived. Marriage embodies a parallel form of this trinity of realities: who my husband is, who I am, and how we carve out in concrete life an abstraction.

Being is the concern of metaphysics.

Yet, while *being* is a metaphysical concept, it is steeped in sensory experience. In the paradox of marriage, two beings who become one flesh participate in a transcendent experience with implications for eternity. Yet, those eternal moments are wrung out through the nitty-gritty of everyday physical intimacies: feeling the heat of another's body next to mine in the bed, drinking from the same bathroom cup, smelling the scent of him on his clothes when I launder them, scooping the tangle of our hair out of the shower drain with bare fingers, tasting the secret seasoning of the food he prepares for me, pulling a splinter from the rough skin of his hand, rolling pennies when it's all we have to buy gas with, hearing his guitar from the next room while I write, watering the holly tree planted in the hole he dug in the yard, feeling him shake in laughter next to me, pouring ginger ale over ice for him when he's sick, chasing the tide together with bare feet on wet sand, hearing the tires of his truck on the stones every evening, sharing the same breeze as we sit in the evening on the front porch, and churning the milk of our bodies into sweet butter on smooth sheets.

The marriage service from *The Book of Common Prayer* of 1662 (a few decades after Donne's death) states that marriage "is an honourable estate, instituted of God in the time of man's innocency, signifying unto us the mystical union that is betwixt Christ and his

Church." In the Christian tradition, marriage is a metaphor that is a picture of the kind of love God has for his people: self-sacrificing and other-focused, spiritual and physical, earthly and transcendent, reasonable and passionate.

Marriage is more than a metaphor: it's a conceit, God's elaboration of himself by means of a human relationship that holds great difference in unified tension. It's God's metaphysical conceit in the poetry of his creation. God is nothing if not a poet. And nothing if not elaborate in both his imagination and composition. *Elaborate,* as the root of the word suggests, means brought about by labor and care, planned with painstaking attention to details or intricate and rich in detail. Just like a metaphysical conceit. To join the unlike—a man and a woman, reason and passion, physical and spiritual—is the work of the poet and of God.

11

Welcoming Wonder: The Poetry of Doubt

A noiseless, patient spider, I mark'd, where, on a
little promontory, it stood, isolated; Mark'd how,
        to explore the vacant, vast surrounding,
It launch'd forth filament, filament, filament,
        out of itself;
Ever unreeling them—ever tirelessly speeding
        them.

And you, O my Soul, where you stand,
Surrounded, surrounded, in measureless oceans
        of space,
Ceaselessly musing, venturing, throwing,—
        seeking the spheres, to connect them;
Till the bridge you will need, be form'd—till the
        ductile anchor hold;
Till the gossamer thread you fling, catch
        somewhere, O my Soul.

—Walt Whitman, "A Noiseless, Patient Spider"

I asked Jesus into my heart before I was 5 years old. It was many
years before I asked him into my mind.

In fairness to myself, it was a long time before I realized that
my mind was a place where Jesus not only needed to be but
wanted to be. The books made this clear to me.

The Book of Matthew records Jesus as saying, "Love the Lord
your God with all your heart and with all your soul and with all
your mind." I didn't accomplish these loves all at once. In fact,
I seem to have followed the order of this verse: first loving Jesus

with my child's heart, a love there in the middle of me, tucked safely away, but hidden in the compartments I'd made for my self and my life. Eventually, that love seeped outward, filling the core of my being, my soul. Why it took so long to fill my mind—to be present in my thinking the same way oxygen is present in my breathing—is the story of these chapters. But it began, if such a thing can be said to have a discrete beginning, in my professor's austere office in the new campus of the state university, after class, when he told me about John Milton, promiscuous reading, and liberty. I'd never had a serious crisis of faith, but I didn't know until I began to love God with my mind that my faith had really been sleeping all these years. John Milton wakened it.

Yet two centuries after Milton, the cultural mood would shift, irrevocably perhaps, from viewing faith as the source of freedom to seeing it as the restrictive chains on human progress. Are we to judge the latter view as right just because it is the newer? I don't think so. Yet, more and more seem to doubt.

As for me, I've never really struggled with doubt—doubt about God's existence or the truth of the bible or the witness and teach-ings of the historic church. But I have faced doubt. I have faced doubt through the disbelief of others, through the questions and honest searching of minds greater than mine, across the ages, on the pages and in the words of the writers I have read. To be sure, I have had questions of my own, and I have grappled with ques-tions alongside others. People sometimes journey from faith to doubt, and I have known such people. Some of these have come back to faith. Others have not. Others I have known began in doubt or unbelief and came to faith. My own faith journey has been slow at times, yet steady and straight. But it has not been a blind faith.

I struggled against God. Not as many do. But still I did, in my own way. I didn't doubt his being. I doubted his ways. I doubted that his ways were better than my ways. I doubted the ways of his people, too. Even so, I wonder more that an airplane can fly than that the God of the universe exists. Granted, my doubt in air-planes is rooted in my ignorance of physics. But might the same apply to our understanding of God? My struggle against God's ways only reinforced my belief in him. After all, one doesn't struggle against something one doesn't believe in. One doesn't rail against someone one thinks does not exist.

Promiscuous reading has humbled me in showing me that "there is nothing new under the sun." As real and as important as any questions I have might be, I've seen that they are not unique to me. There is comfort in this, and chastening, too. Somewhere between universal truth and utter solipsism is a unique self, but the preponderance of that self, like all other selves, is the image of God that all selves share. There's more of him in us—in me—than anything else. Even the ability to doubt him, to struggle against him, to wonder at his ways is rooted in him. Certainty seems bigger than me, skepticism smaller. Wonder is just right.

The line between wonder and doubt is blurry sometimes. In our tendency, like Gulliver, to assume that the measure of things begins and ends with ourselves, to *not know* is easily converted to *can't know*.

This is exactly what happened during the latter half of the nineteenth century. The brightness of that age of progress was beginning to fade. The human, environmental, and social costs of the Industrial Revolution were becoming clearer, and the general sense of optimism of the age—and along with it, faith—was fading. The term *agnosticism,* the belief that definitive knowledge of God's existence is impossible, was coined in these years of growing pessimism by the British biologist Thomas Henry Huxley (brother of Aldous Huxley, author of *Brave New World*). Along with advancing agnosticism, Huxley promoted Charles Darwin's newly developed theory of evolution. Nothing defined the latter half of England's Victorian age more than the way in which Darwin's claims shook the collective faith of Victorian society. The cataclysmic effect of Darwin's ideas on his society is described by historians as a crisis of faith that turned the once-hopeful period into an "age of anxiety" and an "age of doubt." The years surrounding the publication of Darwin's work are the narrow gate through which the age of belief passed into the age of unbelief, not only for England but for the entire Western world within the shockingly brief period of one generation.

Two of the writers who well represent this quantum leap from belief to unbelief are Matthew Arnold and Thomas Hardy. Both were raised in conventionally Christian homes: both ultimately rejected a personal Christian faith and advocated for the larger societal abandonment of that same faith. Yet, despite their vehement repudiation of religious belief, the mood that most characterizes the work of each is, remarkably, profound loss.

Hardy's poems, like his novels, are riddled—in a truly bitter irony—with anger at God for not existing. In his poem "Hap," Hardy asserts the mournful wish that human suffering were caused by the cruelty of God rather than, as he avows, mere chance. The poem expresses the poignant notion that even a malevolent God would be better than no God. For, despite his agnosticism, Hardy recognizes that it is God who provides meaning to human existence, even when that existence is consumed by suffering. The poem opens with the first half of a wistful hypothetical:

> If but some vengeful god would call to me
> From up the sky, and laugh: "Thou suffering thing,
> Know that thy sorrow is my ecstasy,
> That thy love's loss is my hate's profiting!"

Knowing that there was a *reason* for suffering—even if that reason were the mere vengefulness of a cruel deity—would provide a source of strength with which to endure the pain of human suffering even to the point of a defiant death:

> Then would I bear it, clench myself, and die,
> Steeled by the sense of ire unmated;
> Half-eased in that a Powerfuller than I
> Had willed and meted me the tears I shed.

"But not so," says the poem. Rather it is "Crass Casualty"—chance, happenstance, "hap"—that "obstructs sun and rain." Indeed chance and "dicing Time," the poet says, "had as readily strown blisses about my pilgrimage as pain." In other words, suffering and happiness are the simple products of random chance—

as random as are the impersonal forces that set into motion an evolutionary process that is as likely to make one a man as a mollusk. Hardy yearns for even a wicked God in the same way that a battered child ferociously loves even a cruel parent.

Several years after Hardy penned "Hap" in 1866, Nietzsche gave voice to what the culture had already determined, that "God is dead." In accordance with Nietzsche's pronouncement, Hardy commemorated the turn of the century with a poem published on December 31, 1900, "The Darkling Thrush." In this poem, Hardy envisions the closing century as a "corpse" and laments that "every spirit upon earth" seems "fervourless as I." As everywhere in the irreligious Hardy, the language is paradoxically religious: "spirit" and "fervour" are just two examples. The description of the poem's setting is overwhelmed with images of brokenness, death, and decay: a frost that is "spectre-gray," "winter's dregs" that make "desolate the weakening eye of day," "tangled" stems mark the sky "like strings of broken lyres," and a mankind that "haunted nigh." It is remarkable that Hardy wrote this poem as the twentieth century was ushered in, not even knowing what depravities that century had in store for humankind: two world wars marked by devastating casualties, the annihilation of millions of Jews and other "undesirables," acts of genocide across the globe, and the rise of some of the most tyrannical governments human history had ever known. It is not hard for an honest believer to understand the manifold causes of doubt and despair that Hardy both knew and foresaw.

Yet, despite the spiritual death that seems to define the world of the poem, that is not all that is present. For suddenly, there in the midst at the edge of the gray and desolate wood,

> At once a voice arose among
> 　　The bleak twigs overhead
> In a full-hearted evensong
> 　　Of joy illimited;
> An aged thrush, frail, gaunt, and small,
> 　　In blast-beruffled plume
> Had chosen thus to fling his soul

Upon the growing gloom.

While the unexpected appearance of a sign of such joy might en-
liven the soul of the speaker, instead the inexplicable song in the
midst of such sorrow only deepens his sense of loss—and bitterness. The poem concludes:

> So little cause for carolings
>   Of such ecstatic sound
> Was written on terrestrial things
>   Afar or nigh around,
> That I could think there trembled through
>   His happy good-night air
> Some blessed Hope, whereof he knew
>   And I was unaware.

The poet can only wonder at the thrush's seeming knowledge, not
only of "some blessed Hope," but the source of that hope.

Matthew Arnold's poem "Dover Beach" laments the loss of
that hope. Arnold was the epitome of the modern man who pub-
licly professed optimism for the social progress he saw around
him was at odds with his personal sense of melancholy and
mournfulness at the passing of a simpler age. In studying the body
of literature of this time, one can see clearly that this loss of faith
was met first with confusion but then with despair. Arnold be-
speaks such anguish starkly in "Dover Beach." The famous Cliffs
of Dover that guard that beach have for millennia served both literally and figuratively as a source of strength for England, a but-
tress against even the closest and most menacing of enemies.
But the cliffs were unable to provide harbor for an attack greater
than that conveyed by even the fiercest weapons of war—the ero-
sion of the faith that had defined the nation's identity since the
years of the Roman Empire.

Like the cliffs, religion, too, before the age of doubt, was a
source of strength not only to England but to all of civilization.
"Dover Beach" depicts a view of this encompassing "sea of faith"
after it has receded as a result of the skepticism of the modern

age. The dramatic situation of the poem places the speaker at the window of a room at Dover Beach from which he looks out at the night sea. As he watches the gleaming lights on the French coast, the poem opens on a note of futility as he listens to...

> . . . the grating roar
> Of pebbles which the waves draw back, and fling,
> at their return, up the high strand
> Begin, and cease, and then again begin,
> With tremulous cadence slow, and bring
> The eternal note of sadness in.

The speaker eventually contemplates the ebbing sea before him, which reminds him of the "Sea of Faith." Like the literal sea in front of him, this metaphorical sea "was once, too, at the full, and round earth's shore / Lay like the folds of a bright girdle furled." Like the sea, the age of faith, too, is withdrawing with a "melancholy, long withdrawing roar."

In the absence of faith, the speaker turns to the nearest solace he can find: love.

If they can but "be true to one another," then together they can face a world that *seems* "so various, so beautiful, so new." But here the tone of the poem shifts from mere melancholy to near-despair. The fact is, the speaker admits in concluding the poem, that this world, from which faith has retreated,

> Hath really neither joy, nor love, nor light,
> Nor certitude, nor peace, nor help for pain;
> And we are here as on a darkling plain
> Swept with confused alarms of struggle and flight,
> Where ignorant armies clash by night.

Wow.

This is what life with no God is like: no certitude, no peace, no help for pain; a dark, vulnerable existence swept with confused alarms of struggle and flight. Even love seems, according to the poem, merely an illusory substitute for an absent God. And if it is true, as many say, that "God is love," then how can there be love without God? My own faith in God has been uninterrupted from a very young age, so while I've considered intellectually what the absence of God might be like, I've never really felt it. Except through this poem. This—the reality of existence without God, without faith in God—is what the doubter knows. And this knowledge is more powerful than just about anything a preacher ever taught me.

Such poetry of doubt, ironically, helped grow my faith out of my heart and into my mind. Witnessing the logic of doubt in works like these enabled me to work out, inversely, the logic of my faith. A logical faith, I came to see, is all-encompassing, as Hardy depicts it in "Dover Beach." It is not a set of little corrals for keeping in bits of life, but a vast field for planting an entire life. The doubters seemed to see this better than did the believers I knew.

Such yearning for the integrated life of faith permeates another of Matthew Arnold's poems, "The Scholar Gypsy." The speaker of the poem is a modern day man who contemplates the scholar-gypsy of old, a figure made legendary for rejecting the disciplined rigors of Oxford in order to wander the land freely with a group of gypsies. To the poem's speaker—who imagines an encounter centuries later with the still-living scholar-gypsy—this wanderer represents an earlier age, a time "before this strange disease of modern life / With its sick hurry, its divided aims / Its head o'er-taxed, its palsied hearts, was rife." Addressing the scholar-gypsy, the narrator says longingly, "Thou hadst what we [modern men], alas! have not": "Thou hadst one aim, one business, one desire." It was religious faith that gave the scholar-gypsy one aim, one busi-ness, one desire, and as the poem's narrator (not to mention its author) sees it, such faith is no longer possible. The scholar-gypsy, on the other hand, being from that previous age, is "free from the languid doubt" that haunts the modern man and waits hopefully "for the spark from heaven!" But we modern men, the speaker continues,

> Light half-believers of our casual creeds,
>   Who never deeply felt, nor clearly willed,

Whose insight never has borne fruit in deeds,
  Whose vague resolves never have been fulfilled;
   For whom each year we see
Breeds new beginnings, disappointments new;
  Who hesitate and falter life away,
   And lose tomorrow the ground won to-day—
Ah! Do not we wanderer, await it, too?

Both the man of old and the man of today await this spark, but only the ancient scholar-gypsy harbors any hope that the spark will come. Yet, even when people of our contemporary age do have belief, the poem shows, they cannot but be tainted by this "strange disease" of modernism.

  These lines from the poem conjure for me a host of images from the little, country bible-believing churches I grew up in; they echo the countless, endless invitations given at sermon's end each Sunday, in which "with every head bowed and every eye closed" we were urged to raise our hand or to come forward, if not to receive Jesus into our hearts for the first time (never into our minds!), then to renew our commitment to him, or to profess our brokenness, or have an arm put around us in prayer, or simply to kneel once again at the throne of grace. All these earnest entreaties were usually accompanied by the softly-played tune of a sentimental hymn like "Just As I Am." The primary purpose of such a call, of course, was to confess the faith and receive salvation. But even those who had already so done were encouraged time and again to come forward for renewal or recommitment.

  It seemed to me like a revolving door, these endless altar calls, a tradition that allowed people to make decisions that no one seemed to expect would actually be kept, since next week and the week after and the week after that would come yet another opportunity to get things right, once and for all (or at least until next time). So just as firmly as I believed in the efficacy of a prayer for salvation, I firmly refused to raise my hand or shuffle forward or drop a tear along with those sniffling beside me, no matter how many times the preacher taunted those of us remaining (was I the only one?) with our heads still bowed and eyes still closed with those tempting words, "I see that hand in the back" and "I see that one over there." I knew that Jesus had saved me because I had asked him into my heart, and I didn't need organ music or an eloquent preacher to get right with God, so what was the point?

As the speaker in the poem observes, in this age, "Each year we see breeds new beginnings, disappointments new; who hesitate and falter life away, and lose tomorrow the ground won today." This is, according to the poem, the disease of modern life. It is not that we can no longer have belief, though doing so is much harder in the context of modern skepticism. But even in possession of it, we modern people of faith tend to be but "light half-believers of our casual creeds."

I didn't feel like a "light half-believer," although I felt like I couldn't be myself in church. That I couldn't talk there about the music I listened to or the things my friends and I talked about or the books I read. As a Baptist, I was taught that once a person puts her faith in Christ, her salvation cannot be lost. "Once saved, always saved," it was said. There was so much talk about heaven and eternal life that I began to wonder what was the point of life on this earth. If this life on earth were just a waystation on the road to eternity, a mere tripping the light fantastic, why were we even here? Of what use was eternal salvation without a salvation for each day? Perhaps it's that tenuous connection between heaven and earth that makes even surefire Baptists seem to doubt their salvation so often. We who believe—who want to believe—are asked to believe much, caught as we feel we are between two ill-fitted worlds.

It was many years before I learned that repentance means a change in thinking, not just a change in heart. During those restless years of unrepentance, I would lie awake at night and think about the things I was choosing to do—all of them variations of my failing to live up to the expectations I had been given and, deep down, had accepted for my life. But I didn't desire to change a thing. I wanted to do what I wanted to do, during that dark night of the will. But, St. Augustine cried out to God in his Confessions, "Thou hast made us for thyself, O Lord, and our hearts are restless until they find their rest in thee."

Some nights I would rock myself to sleep. Some nights I would sing over and over in my head a portion of a song I had heard as a little girl and turned into a kind of prayer. And some nights I would really pray. I asked God to give me the desire to desire to change. That was as close as I was willing to meet him, and no further.

And he met me where I was. In the books.

DISCUSSION QUESTIONS

Chapter 1 • Books Promiscuously Read:
John Milton's *Areopagitica*

1. What books do you remember from your childhood?

2. How did these books influence you?

3. What criteria do you use to decide which books to read and which not to read? Has this changed over the course of your life? If so, how?

4. Are "good" literature and "popular" literature the same thing? Why or why not? Is what you like to read necessarily "good" literature and if not is that okay?

5. Do you think books are a good source for discovering truth? How so?

6. Do you agree with Milton's view about the strength of truth to overcome falsehood? Are there some ideas that should be censored? Or is truth always strong enough to overpower wrong ideas?

Chapter 2 • The Life-Giving Power of Words:
Charlotte's Web

1. What role did animals or pets have in your childhood? What role do they have now?

2. Why are books about animals so appealing to young people?

3. What are some examples of the power of words or names?

4. How have the words spoken about you by others influenced your life, whether positively or negatively?

5. Have you ever felt directly responsible for the suffering of another? How did you cope with that burden?

Chapter 3 • God of the Awkward, the Freckled, and the Strange: Gerard Manley Hopkins' "Pied Beauty"

1. What roles have the outcasts in your life played? Have you ever been an outcast?

2. Does every community have outcasts? Why is this so?

3. How can communities be more accommodating to "the awkward" and "the strange"?

4. What are some unexpected sources of beauty that you have encountered?

5. How is the power of the strange different from the power of beauty? How is it the same?

Chapter 4 • The Magic of Story: *Great Expectations*

1. Did you have a teacher who influenced your life more than any other? How so?

2. What book from your childhood held the most "magic" for you? Why?

3. Is there a book you have loved that others around you just didn't understand or love as much?

4. What are some examples of the modern day tendency to divide our lives and ourselves into compartments? How can this be overcome? Should it be?

5. Is your spiritual life more connected to your emotions or your intellect or both?

6. Have you had experiences that caused you to turn away from religious groups or institutions?

7. Who in your life has been as steadfast and loyal as Joe was to Pip, even when you have not deserved it?

Chapter 5 • Beholding is Becoming: *Jane Eyre*

1. What character from literature do you most identify with? Why?

2. What temptations have you had to overcome on your journey to being yourself?

3. Is becoming yourself more about discovering who you are or who you aren't? Or both?

4. Is the modern individual more a creation of the self or of social forces? How so?

5. Have you ever been rejected from a group you longed to be part of? How did you cope with such an experience?

6. Have you ever used journaling or writing to overcome life challenges?

7. How does journaling or writing help one to develop as an individual?

8. How do books help one to become oneself?

Chapter 6 • The Only Thing Between Me and Tragedy: *Tess of the D'Urbervilles*

1. Writing at the end of the 19th century, Thomas Hardy explored the double standard of sexual morality that prevailed during that time. How much has that double standard changed today?

2. Have you ever hesitated to read a book, like the college student who found reading *Tess of the D'Urbervilles* too painful because of her own similar experience? Can reading about similar experiences be helpful or hurtful in our attempts to overcome them? Why or why not?

3. Have sex education and more openness about sexuality helped to prevent situations like the one Tess experienced in the novel? What about that experienced by the author's mother?

4. How can the blindness that prevents us from seeing others as they really are be tragic? Can you think of examples of this from other works of literature or from real life?

5. Have you ever experienced illumination or insight about a person that transformed you or the relationship?

6. Have you ever felt God's presence or intervention in your life—only to ignore it? What was the dynamic there?

Chapter 7 • Sex, Symbol, and Satire: *Gulliver's Travels*

1. A symbol is something that represents something else. This chapter discusses symbols of sex and the power of those symbols. What are other kinds of powerful symbols in our society?

2. What are examples of false symbols prevalent today?

3. What is something important about which your views, values, and beliefs have changed or matured over time?

4. An 18th century cleric seems like an unlikely source of reliable knowledge about sex. Have you ever learned something from a surprising source?

5. Satire is the ridicule of folly for the purpose of correction. Name some examples of satire in film, art, TV, and literature.

6. Is satire an effective way to bring about correction or change?

Chapter 8 • Know Thyself: *Death of a Salesman*

1. What are some of the ways a person comes to know him or herself?

2. An ancient saying is that "adversity introduces a man to himself." How do painful life experiences help you to discover who you are?

3. What are some of the most important things one should know about oneself? Is the same thing as "finding oneself"? Why or why not?

4. How did you learn what your true calling in life was? Is there only one calling? Can one's calling change throughout the course of one's life?

5. How important is one's work to one's identity? How much is what one does part of who one is?

6. What is the American Dream? Is it a good dream? Or has it been corrupted?

7. How did Willy Loman's noble pursuit of the American Dream get off course?

8. What role do family and community play in shaping views and attitudes about work?

Chapter 9 • The Fate of the Romantic: *Madame Bovary*

1. The author's view of the romantic worldview is negative. Do you agree or disagree with this assessment? Does a romantic worldview have positive aspects that are overlooked here?

2. What are some other examples of romantic thinking today? What are the sources of these idealized images?

3. What is the appeal of romanticism? Of realism?

4. How have "fairy tale" versions of life you might have once believed been challenged and changed by real life?

5. How can we do a better job of advancing the idea that real life, even with disappointments, is better than fantasy?

6. Is there any book you've read that has transformed your thinking and life as *Madame Bovary* did for the author?

Chapter 10 • Real Love is Like a Compass: John Donne's Metaphysical Poetry

1. This chapter presents a version of real love that is markedly different from the romanticized view of love in the previous chapter. What are some of the differences?

2. Is there a place for "romance" in real love?

3. How does the author distinguish between romantic love and transcendent love? Is there overlap between them?

4. What are some simple, concrete everyday events or things that bring pleasure to your everyday life?

Chapter 11 • Welcoming Wonder: The Poetry of Doubt

1. What do you see as the relationship between faith and the mind?

2. The author writes, "Certainty seems bigger than me, skepticism smaller. Wonder is just right." Do you agree with this statement? Why or why not?

3. There are many kinds of doubt that one can experience, not only the religious doubt that is the subject of this chapter. What other kinds of doubt do people experience? What are the ways in which these can be overcome?

4. Many of the chapters in the book, including this one, describe aspects of life in previous centuries. Which aspects of those eras discussed in the book seem most different from today? What aspects are unchanged?

5. Do you relate more with the doubt expressed by the poets in this chapter or with the author's faith?

6. What are the unexpected places in life that where you have found your faith strengthened?

7. What are the sources of continuing wonder for you?

ACKNOWLEDGMENTS

This book owes its existence most of all to my students, many of whom have heard the ideas and stories contained here in my classes and in our conversations. It is my students who believed in this book long enough and strongly enough to bring it into being. Some of those who cheered me on, listened to readings, read chapters, and supported this project in various other ways include Brandon Ambrosino, John Carl, Amber Forcey, Alaina Hohnarth, Ryan Knight, Lauren Lund, Kyra Marken, Andy Beth Miller, and Amy Rickards. It's been a long time in coming, and all of you have been there along the way.

Thanks to Randy Scott Carroll for letting me borrow his name.

I'm ever appreciative of the painstaking, skillful work of my research assistant, Keegan Bradford.

To the friends who lent eyes, ears, minds, and hearts during the long drafting phase, I am exceedingly grateful: Christine Bradford, Deal Hudson, and Cheryl Smith.

And for those students who have surpassed the teacher, who have taught me eminently more than I have taught them and have contributed immeasurably to this project, I have inexpressible gratitude: Samuel Loncar and Nick Olson.

Thank you to Laura Barkat for seeing potential and to David Wheeler for bringing that potential out so patiently and expertly.

And I am especially grateful to my husband and parents for their loving support as I endlessly wrote, but even more, for letting me share some of their stories, which have made my story what it is.

END NOTES

Chapter 1

page 20.   "And this is the benefit that may be had by books promiscuously read": John Milton, *Areopagitica* (Boston: Houghton Mifflin, 1998), p. 1006-1007. Language modernized by this author.

page 22.   "Read any books": Eusebius quoted in John Milton, *Areopagitica* (Boston: Houghton Mifflin, 1998), p. 1005.

page 22.   "test all things": 1 Thessalonians 5:21, *King James Bible* (Thomas Nelson Bibles, 1982).

page 22.   "Well knows he who uses to consider": John Milton, *Areopagitica* (Boston: Houghton Mifflin, 1998), p. 1015.

page 23.   "Captivate...under a perpetual childhood": John Milton, *Areopagitica* (Boston: Houghton Mifflin, 1998), p. 1006.

page 23.   "What wisdom can there be to choose": John Milton, *Areopagitica* (Boston: Houghton Mifflin, 1998), p. 1006.

page 23.   "What praise for 'a fugitive and cloistered virtue'": John Milton, *Areopagitica* (Boston: Houghton Mifflin, 1998), p. 1006.

page 23.   "Those 'who imagine to remove sin'": John Milton, *Areopagitica* (Boston: Houghton Mifflin, 1998), p. 1010.

page 23.   "Best books...to a naughty mind": John Milton, *Areopagitica* (Boston: Houghton Mifflin, 1998), p. 1005.

page 23.   "Bad books...to a discreet and judicious reader": John Milton, *Areopagitica* (Boston: Houghton Mifflin, 1998), p. 1005.

page 23.   "For who knows not that Truth is strong": John Milton, *Areopagitica* (Boston: Houghton Mifflin, 1998), p. 1021.

Chapter 2

page 31.   "do away with": E. B. White, *Charlotte's Web* (New York: HarperTrophy, 1980), p. 1.

page 39.   "grasshoppers, choice beetles, moths...I don't really eat them": E. B. White, *Charlotte's Web* (New York: HarperTrophy, 1980), p. 39.

page 40. "Why not?": ibid.

page 40. "that he was mistaken about Charlotte": E. B. White, *Charlotte's Web* (New York: HarperTrophy, 1980), p. 41.

page 42. "Some pig": E. B. White, *Charlotte's Web* (New York: HarperTrophy, 1980), p. 79.

page 42. "That doesn't make a particle of difference": E. B. White, *Charlotte's Web* (New York: HarperTrophy, 1980), p. 89.

page 42. "everything possible to make himself glow": E. B. White, *Charlotte's Web* (New York: HarperTrophy, 1980), p. 114.

page 42. "Actually...I feel radiant": E. B. White, *Charlotte's Web* (New York: HarperTrophy, 1980), p. 101.

page 42. "humble": E. B. White, *Charlotte's Web* (New York: HarperTrophy, 1980), p. 140.

page 43. "It's not often that someone comes along": E. B. White, *Charlotte's Web* (New York: HarperTrophy, 1980), p. 184.

Chapter 4

page 59. "It will be proved that he is hardly even a caricaturist": G. K. Chesterton, "Appreciations and Criticisms of the Works of Charles Dickens" found in *Charles Dickens; A Critical Study* (New York: E. P. Dutton & Co., 1911), Accessed online at Forgottonbooks.com, p. xv. <http://www.forgottenbooks.org/info/9781451000528>

page 59. "I found him to be a dry man": Charles Dickens, *Great Expectations* (New York: Bantam Books, 1986), p. 179.

page 59. "His mouth was such a post-office of a mouth": Charles Dickens, *Great Expectations* (New York: Bantam Books, 1986), p. 180.

page 60. "By degrees, Wemmick got dryer and harder": Charles Dickens, *Great Expectations* (New York: Bantam Books, 1986), p. 220.

page 60. "Walworth is one place": Charles Dickens, *Great Expectations* (New York: Bantam Books, 1986), p. 310.

page 63. "When the soul does not yet know any abyss": Georg Lukacs, *Preface to The Theory of the Novel* (Cambridge: MIT Press, 1971), p. 30.

page 63.   "Why here's a J and a O": Charles Dickens, *Great Expectations* (New York: Bantam Books, 1986), p. 46.

page 64.   "Give me…a good book": Charles Dickens, *Great Expectations* (New York: Bantam Books, 1986), p. 47.

page 65.   "always aided and comforted me": Charles Dickens, *Great Expectations* (New York: Bantam Books, 1986), p. 25.

page 66.   "Home had never been a very pleasant place": Charles Dickens, *Great Expectations* (New York: Bantam Books, 1986), p. 112.

page 67.   "there was a constant tendency in all these people": Charles Dickens, *Great Expectations* (New York: Bantam Books, 1986), p. 493.

page 68.   "You cannot see my face": Exodus 33:20, *New American Standard Bible* (The Lockman Foundation, 1960, 1962, 1963, 1968, 1971, 1973, 1975, 1977, 1995).

page 69.   Exodus 33:18-22, *New American Standard Bible* (The Lockman Foundation, 1960, 1962, 1963, 1968, 1971, 1973, 1975, 1977, 1995).

page 69   Footnote to Exodus 33:22: R. C. Sproul, ed. *The Reformation Study Bible: English Standard Version* (Orlando, FL: Ligonier Ministries, 2005).

Chapter 5

page 73.   "I will show you a heroine": Elizabeth Gaskell, *The Life of Charlotte Brontë* (Published 1857, Accessed online at Classiclit.about.com May 16, 2012). <http://classiclit.about.com/library/bl-etexts/egaskell/bl-egaskell-cbronte-16.htm>

page 74.   "I am not an angel": Charlotte Brontë, *Jane Eyre* (New York: Barnes & Noble Classics, 2003), p. 301.

page 78.   "Happy families are all alike": Leo Tolstoy, *Anna Karenina* (New York: Bantam Books, 2006), p. 1.

page 81.   "Eliza, John, and Georgiana": Charlotte Brontë, *Jane Eyre* (New York: Barnes & Noble Classics, 2003), p. 1.

page 81.   "contented, happy, little": Charlotte Brontë, *Jane Eyre* (New York: Barnes & Noble Classics, 2003), p. 1.

page 81.   "red room…breathed his last ": Charlotte Brontë, *Jane Eyre* (New York: Barnes & Noble Classics, 2003), p. 6.

page 82.   "I resisted all the way": Charlotte Brontë, *Jane Eyre* (New York: Barnes & Noble Classics, 2003), p. 6.

page 82.   The preface to the 1988 publication of Jane Eyre: Joyce Carol Oates, *Jane Eyre: An Introduction* (New York: Bantam Classic, 1988).

page 82.   "bleak shores": Charlotte Brontë, *Jane Eyre* (New York: Barnes & Noble Classics, 2003), p. 2.

page 83.   "like a murderer": Charlotte Brontë, *Jane Eyre* (New York: Barnes & Noble Classics, 2003), p. 5.

page 85.   "This world is pleasant": Charlotte Brontë, *Jane Eyre* (New York: Barnes & Noble Classics, 2003), p. 86-87.

page 86.   "Do you think?": Charlotte Brontë, *Jane Eyre* (New York: Barnes & Noble Classics, 2003), p. 294.

page 86.   "My future husband was becoming my whole world": Charlotte Brontë, *Jane Eyre* (New York: Barnes & Noble Classics, 2003), p. 318-319.

page 87.   "Conventionality is not morality": Charlotte Brontë, the preface to *Jane Eyre* (New York: Barnes & Noble Classics, 2003), p. xlvi.

page 88.   "What shall I do, Jane?": Charlotte Brontë, *Jane Eyre* (New York: Barnes & Noble Classics, 2003), p. 367.

page 88.   "Who in the world cares for you?...Still indomitable was the reply": Charlotte Brontë, *Jane Eyre* (New York: Barnes & Noble Classics, 2003), p. 368.

page 91.   "God and nature intended you": Charlotte Brontë, *Jane Eyre* (New York: Barnes & Noble Classics, 2003), p. 468.

page 91.   "natures are at variance": Charlotte Brontë, *Jane Eyre* (New York: Barnes & Noble Classics, 2003), p. 475.

page 91.   "I scorn your idea of love": Charlotte Brontë, *Jane Eyre* (New York: Barnes & Noble Classics, 2003), p. 475.

page 91.   "I felt veneration for St. John": Charlotte Brontë, *Jane Eyre* (New York: Barnes & Noble Classics, 2003), p. 486.

page 93.   "The most alarming revolution": Elsie B. Mitchie, *The introduction to Charlotte Brontë's Jane Eyre: A Case Book* (Oxford University Press, 2006), p. 15.

Chapter 6

page 96.   "Maiden No More": Thomas Hardy, title of chapter XII of *Tess of the d'Ubervilles* (London: Penguin Books, 1998), p. 75.

page 96.   "A pure woman faithfully presented": Thomas Hardy, subtitle of *Tess of the d'Ubervilles* (London: Penguin Books, 1998), p. 1.

page 99.   Interview with Thomas Hardy: Margaret R. Higgonet, *Introduction to Tess of the D'Ubervilles* (London: Penguin Books, 1998), p. xx.

page 99.   "more sinned against than sinning": Thomas Hardy, *Tess of the d'Ubervilles* (London: Penguin Books, 1998), p. 232

page 100.   "…he now began to discredit the old appraisements": Thomas Hardy, *Tess of the d'Ubervilles* (London: Penguin Books, 1998), p. 340.

page 103.   "I thought, Angel, that you loved me": Thomas Hardy, *Tess of the d'Ubervilles* (London: Penguin Books, 1998), p. 228-229.

page 103.   "Blindness is 'the most unforgivable crime in fiction'": Azar Nafisi, *Reading Lolita in Tehran* (New York: Random House Books, 2004), p. 224.

page 103.   "Evil, in most great fiction": Azar Nafisi, *Reading Lolita in Tehran* (New York: Random House Books, 2004), p. 315.

page 104   "see[ing] through a glass darkly": 1 Corinthians 13:12, *New King James Bible* (Thomas Nelson Bibles, 1982).

page 104.   "In them, and in them alone": Arthur Miller, "Tragedy and the Common Man (published online by *The New York Times*, February 27, 1949), <http://www.nytimes.com/books/00/11/12/specials/miller-com mon.html>.

page 104.   "This prophet simply and 'plainly' tells Angel": Thomas Hardy, *Tess of the d'Ubervilles* (London: Penguin Books, 1998), p. 341.

page 105.   "Too late, too late": Thomas Hardy, *Tess of the d'Ubervilles* (London: Penguin Books, 1998), p. 378.

page 106.   "I cannot help associating your decline": Thomas Hardy, *Tess of the d'Ubervilles* (London: Penguin Books, 1998), p. 232.

page 106.   "But, might some say": Thomas Hardy, *Tess of the d'Ubervilles* (London: Penguin Books, 1998), p. 74.

page 111. "Forgive me as you are forgiven": Thomas Hardy, *Tess of the d'Urbervilles* (London: Penguin Books, 1998), p. 228.

page 112. "O mother, my mother": Thomas Hardy, *Tess of the d'Urbervilles* (London: Penguin Books, 1998), p. 82.

page 114. "a parable of the tragedy": James Townsend, "Thomas Hardy: The Tragedy of a Life Without Christ" (*Journal of the Grace Evangelical Society*, 10.18: 1997).

Chapter 7

page 122. "...that every soldier in his march": Jonathan Swift, *Gulliver's Travels* (New York: Random House, 1991), p. 39.

page 124. This concept is discussed in detail by Jean Beaudrillard in his work *Simulacra and Simulation* (Ann Arbor, MI: the University of Michigan Press, 1994).

page 126. "the death of sex": ibid.

page 130. "Satire is a sort of glass": Jonathan Swift, the *Preface to The Battle of the Books* (Middlesex: The Echo Library, 2007), p. 1.

page 134. "into fits...Celia": Jonathan Swift, "The Lady's Dressing Room" (Accessed online at PoetryFoundation.com July 19, 2012). <http://www.poetryfoundation.org/poem/180934>

page 134. "Lovers for the sake of celestial converse": Jonathan Swift, Works of Jonathan Swift (Published in 1774, Accessed online at Google Books), p. 190. <http://books.google.com/books?id=sbArAQAAMAAJ&pg=PA190&lpg=PA190&dq#v=onepage&q&f=false>

page 135. "At the time I am writing": Jonathan Swift, *Gulliver's Travels* (New York: Random House, 1991), p. 311.

Chapter 8

page 148. "Well-liked": Arthur Miller, *Death of a Salesman* (New York: Penguin Classics, 1998), p. 18.

page 148. "put on his green velvet slippers": Arthur Miller, *Death of a Salesman* (New York: Penguin Classics, 1998), p.61

page 148. "selling was the greatest career": ibid.

page 148.   "died the death of a salesman": ibid.

page 149.   "He had the wrong dreams": Arthur Miller, *Death of a Salesman* (New York: Penguin Classics, 1998), p.111.

page 150.   "Even your wants": Gene Edward Veith, *God At Work* (Wheaton, IL: Crossway, 2011), p. 52.

page 150.   "Our vocation is not something we choose": Gene Edward Veith, *God At Work* (Wheaton, IL: Crossway, 2011), p.47.

page 150.   "a function of the particular gifts": Gene Edward Veith, *God At Work* (Wheaton, IL: Crossway, 2011), p.54.

page 152.   "There were a lot of nice days": Arthur Miller, *Death of a Salesman* (New York: Penguin Classics, 1998), p.110.

page 152.   "Yeah. He was a happy man": ibid.

page 152.   "snakes and rabbits": Arthur Miller, *Death of a Salesman* (New York: Penguin Classics, 1998), p.35.

page 152.   "The grass don't grow anymore": Arthur Miller, *Death of a Salesman* (New York: Penguin Classics, 1998), p. 6.

page 153.   "a very great and wild-hearted man": Arthur Miller, *Death of a Salesman* (New York: Penguin Classics, 1998), p. 34.

page 153.   "We should be mixing cement": Arthur Miller, *Death of a Salesman* (New York: Penguin Classics, 1998), p. 44.

page 153.   "How can they whip cheese": Arthur Miller, *Death of a Salesman* (New York: Penguin Classics, 1998), p. 7.

page 153.   "nothing's planted": Arthur Miller, *Death of a Salesman* (New York: Penguin Classics, 1998), p. 98.

page 154.   "The man don't know": Arthur Miller, *Death of a Salesman* (New York: Penguin Classics, 1998), p. 104.

page 154.   "We never told the truth": ibid.

page 154.   "hot air...all I want is out there": Arthur Miller, *Death of a Salesman* (New York: Penguin Classics, 1998), p. 105.

Chapter 9

page 163.   "When she went to confession": Gustave Flaubert, *Madame Bovary, A Norton Critical Edition,* trans. Paul de Man (New York: W. W. Norton & Company, 1965), p. 25.

page 163.   "Accustomed to the quieter aspects of life": Gustave Flaubert, *Madame Bovary, A Norton Critical Edition,* trans. Paul de Man (New York: W. W. Norton & Company, 1965), p. 25-6.

page 163.   "Kitch causes two tears": Milan Kundera, *The Unbearable Lightness of Being* (New York: HarperCollins, 2004), p. 251.

page 163.   "Emma was secretly pleased": Gustave Flaubert, *Madame Bovary, A Norton Critical Edition,* trans. Paul de Man (New York: W. W. Norton & Company, 1965), p. 27.

page 164.   "were all about love": Gustave Flaubert, *Madame Bovary, A Norton Critical Edition,* trans. Paul de Man (New York: W. W. Norton & Company, 1965), p. 26.

page 164.   "I have come to love": ibid.

page 169.   "she thought herself in love": Gustave Flaubert, *Madame Bovary, A Norton Critical Edition,* trans. Paul de Man (New York: W. W. Norton & Company, 1965), p. 24.

page 169.   "Why could not she lean over balconies": Gustave Flaubert, *Madame Bovary, A Norton Critical Edition,* trans. Paul de Man (New York: W. W. Norton & Company, 1965), p. 29 & 31.

page 170.   "the greater became the gulf": ibid.

page 172.   "veneration for illustrious or unhappy women": Gustave Flaubert, *Madame Bovary, A Norton Critical Edition,* trans. Paul de Man (New York: W. W. Norton & Company, 1965), p. 26.

page 173.   "He was happy then": Gustave Flaubert, *Madame Bovary, A Norton Critical Edition,* trans. Paul de Man (New York: W. W. Norton & Company, 1965), p. 23.

page 173.   "Trotted over the country roads": Gustave Flaubert, *Madame Bovary, A Norton Critical Edition,* trans. Paul de Man (New York: W. W. Norton & Company, 1965), p. 43.

page 173.   "waiting in her heart": Gustave Flaubert, *Madame Bovary, A Norton Critical Edition,* trans. Paul de Man (New York: W. W. Norton & Company,

1965), p. 44.

page 174.   "It is a girl!": Gustave Flaubert, *Madame Bovary, A Norton Critical Edition,* trans. Paul de Man (New York: W. W. Norton & Company, 1965), p. 63.

page 174.   "for manures!": Gustave Flaubert, *Madame Bovary, A Norton Critical Edition,* trans. Paul de Man (New York: W. W. Norton & Company, 1965), p. 107.

page 174.   "Then she recalled the heroines": Gustave Flaubert, *Madame Bovary, A Norton Critical Edition,* trans. Paul de Man (New York: W. W. Norton & Company, 1965), p. 117.

page 175.   "delight in his image": Gustave Flaubert, *Madame Bovary, A Norton Critical Edition,* trans. Paul de Man (New York: W. W. Norton & Company, 1965), p. 77.

page 175.   "Ah! It is but a little thing": Gustave Flaubert, *Madame Bovary, A Norton Critical Edition,* trans. Paul de Man (New York: W. W. Norton & Company, 1965), p. 230.

page 176.   "with a tenderness in his eyes": Gustave Flaubert, *Madame Bovary, A Norton Critical Edition,* trans. Paul de Man (New York: W. W. Norton & Company, 1965), p. 231.

Chapter 10

page 180.   "John Donne, Anne Donne , Un-done": John Donne in a letter to his wife. John Stubbs, *John Donne: The Reformed Soul* (New York: W. W. Norton, 2006), page 154.

page 182.   "Batter my heart": John Donne, "Holy Sonnet 14: Batter my heart" (Accessed online at PoetryFoundation.com July 19, 2012). <http://www.poetryfoundation.org/poem/173362>

page 182.   "Death, be not proud": John Donne, "Holy Sonnet 10: Death, be not proud" (Accessed online at PoetryFoundation.com July 19, 2012). <http://www.poetryfoundation.org/poem/173363>

page 184.   "they are two so": John Donne, "A Valediction: Forbidding Mourning" (Accessed online at PoetryFoundation.com July 19, 2012). <http://www.poetryfoundation.org/poem/173387>

page 185.   "Thy soul...the fixed foot": ibid.

page 185.   "Such wilt thou be": ibid.

Chapter 11

page 189.   "Love the Lord your God": Matthew 22:37, *New International Version* (International Bible Society, 1973, 1978, 1984).

page 191.   "new under the sun": Ecclesiastes 1:9, *New International Version* (International Bible Society, 1973, 1978, 1984).

page 192.   "If but some vengeful god": Thomas Hardy, "Hap" (Accessed online at PoetryFoundation.com July 19, 2012). <http://www.poetryfounda tion.org/poem/175582>

page 192.   "Then would I bear it": ibid.

page 192.   'dicing Time": ibid.

page 193.   "every spirit upon earth": Thomas Hardy, "The Darkling Thrush" (Accessed online at PoetryFoundation.com July 19, 2012). <http://www.poetryfoundation.org/poem/173590>

page 193.   "spectre-gray": ibid.

page 193.   "At once a voice arose": ibid.

page 194.   "So little cause for carolings": ibid.

page 195.   "...the grating roar": Matthew Arnold, "Dover Beach" (Accessed on-line at PoetryFoundation.com July 19, 2012). <http://www.poetry foundation.org/poem/172844>

page 195.   "was once, too, at the full": ibid.

page 195.   "melancholy, long withdrawing roar": ibid.

page 195.   "seems… be true to one another": ibid.

page 195.   "Hath really neither joy, nor love, nor light": ibid.

page 196.   "Before this strange disease": Matthew Arnold, " The Scholar-Gipsy" (Accessed online at PoetryFoundation.com July 19, 2012). <http://www.poetryfoundation.org/poem/172862>

page 196.   "Thou hadst what we": ibid.

page 196.   "free from the languid doubt": ibid.

page 196.   "Light half-believers": ibid.

ALSO FROM T. S. POETRY PRESS

Rumors of Water: Thoughts on Creativity & Writing,
by L.L. Barkat

A few brave writers pull back the curtain to show us their creative process. Annie Dillard did this. So did Hemingway. Now L.L. Barkat has given us a thoroughly modern analysis of writing. Practical, yes, but also a gentle uncovering of the art of being a writer.

— Gordon Atkinson, author *Turtles All the Way Down*

Delicate Machinery Suspended, **by Anne M. Doe Overstreet**

Anne Overstreet employs the skilled chemistry that swells the words back into realities so startling and new that no object or person remains unchanged.

—Luci Shaw, author of *Harvesting Fog*

These poems shimmer with gossamer lightness but also possess the strength and sinews of hard-won wisdom and what Henry James called felt life.

—Gregory Wolfe, Editor at *Image Journal*

"I look up to take it in," Anne Overstreet writes, and so she does. She takes it all in, and gives it back to us.

—John Wilson, Editor at *Books & Culture*

All T. S. Poetry Press titles are available online in e-book and print editions. Print editions also available through Ingram.

Follow T. S. Poetry Press on Facebook at
https://www.facebook.com/tspoetrypress

If you blog about *Booked,* please feel free to
share your post link on our T. S. Poetry Press Facebook Wall.
We'd love to hear your thoughts.

Made in the USA
Charleston, SC
04 April 2013